WITHDRAWN

Collectible Kay Finch

W9-CEK-187

Ka

Biography
Identification
Values

Devin Frick
Jean Frick
Richard Martinez

COLLECTOR BOOKS
A Division of Schroeder Publishing

The current values of this book should be used only as a guide. They are not intended to set prices, which vary from one section of the country to another. Auction prices as well as dealer prices vary greatly and are affected by condition as well as demand. Neither the Authors nor the Publisher assumes responsibility for any losses that might be incurred as a result of consulting this guide.

Searching for a Publisher?

We are always looking for knowledgeable people considered to be experts within their fields. If you feel that there is a real need for a book on your collectible subject and have a large comprehensive collection, contact Collector Books.

Cover Design: Terri Stalions
Book Design: Donna Ballard

On the Cover:

Clockwise from top right, Stallion, #213; Perky poodle, #5419;
Ambrosia, #155; Persian couple, #5160 and #5161; Briar
Rose dinnerware; #4634; Coach Dog, #159.

Contents

Acknowledgments

To us this book was a labor of love and we wish to thank the many who opened their doors and hearts to share their memories, thoughts, recollections, and collections. Everyone we contacted was so helpful and outgoing, and this book would not have been possible without their involvement.

Many people who knew the Finches were generous with their time, knowledge, and contacts. Speaking with them was one of the great pleasures of this research, and we want particularly to thank Pat Hadden Chapman, Lutie Belle Williamson Lindeman, Stan Skee, Iola F. Skee, Margaret Hiner, Dorothy Lombard, Ruby Buchanan Jordan, Jane Holmes Ross, Betsy Rabbitt Pomeroy, Maureen Rischard, Lois Hopkins, Jessie Hill, and Jackie Smiley.

We are extremely grateful to everyone mentioned above and will not forget that all of them offered great amounts of support and encouragement. Thanks to those who lent their time, talents and collections, Sharlene and Jim Beckwith, Chris and Anna Ottzen, Roberta Tripoli, Tamara Hodge of Ceramic Care Unit, David C. Michaels, Jim Andrus, the Santa Ana Public Library, The Miss Pearl Chase Collection of the Santa Barbara Public Library, the Newport Beach Public Library and Lisa Stroup and the staff at Collector Books. Thanks to Maxine Nelson for introducing us in 1978 to the rediscovery of California pottery and to Jack Chipman for letting us in on the wide world of California ceramics.

Our gratitude goes to Frances Finch Webb and her husband Jack Webb, who gave their "blessing," for their constant help and dedication in seeing this project through. Thank you for making our research easier with the stories, advertisements, photos, and a wonderful personal collection, including Kay's one-of-a-kind pieces. Special thanks go to Rick Flynn for his fine photography.

One must understand that in the development and research of any particular subject, help from many individuals, including family, friends, workers, and acquaintances, had to be sought. Unfortunately we were unable to reach everyone who knew or worked for Kay Finch and regret any unintentional omissions or untold stories.

This book was written as a tribute to an outstanding artist and woman. Ceramically speaking, it's also a record of the manner in which the pieces displayed in the book were born. Further, in the area of social history, we hope that we have been able to capture the spirit of the World War II and postwar eras in Southern California during which these ceramics were produced.

Careful attention to detail and a strong dedication to their work inspired the artisans who worked at the Finch Studio. Now, through their memories, memorabilia and artifacts, we are all granted a look back in time to California's "Golden Age of Pottery." We wanted very much to make this journey while the window of opportunity was available. Too soon, it will be closed forever.

Preface

Each of us was born and grew up in the state of California and one of us fondly remembers as a child driving with her parents down a very long and dusty road, way out into the "country," far away from big city Los Angeles. Those Sunday drives eventually led to the rocky coastline of the Pacific Ocean and the small village communities of Laguna Beach and Corona del Mar. The family would play in the water, picnic on the beach, and visit the array of pottery and cottage industry shops along Pacific Coast Highway on those warm, sunny afternoons.

One of the shops a bit down the road had a display of brightly painted, pastel animals, all done in curls and swirls. These fantastic creations lined shelves that stretched far to the ceiling. The figurines were grouped and displayed in such a beautiful setting overlooking the ocean that you felt as if you were in a dream. With so many sculptures from which to choose, which one would we take home? Cats and kittens were the girl's favorite, so several were purchased to add to her collection and to remember that very special day and place.

Those cats stayed on her dresser for years with one being added to the growing family every now and then from other trips and as gifts.

Those cats had an effect years later when I was putting together a small exhibit on California pottery at a local museum in Anaheim. Vernon Kilns and Brayton Laguna had always intrigued me, but the work of this one woman artist from my childhood experience was indeed masterful and there was so much more work than just cats. Research uncovered a gold mine of information, memorabilia and ceramics from this local artist and I was interested in sharing this important information with others intrigued by Kay Finch ceramics.

We spoke eventually to friends and employees and

The first curlicue Cats, early 1940s. Mehitabel, Hannibal and Jezebel.

began gathering information about this Orange County artist, by way of El Paso, Texas. The work began to grow and became more interesting as we progressed with our research. It has come to be compiled into this book saluting Kay Finch and her achievements both in her art and in her life.

These sculptures made and still make us smile when we look at them. They are both humorous and serious and all are in every way professionally done. The ceramics pictured here were found in antique stores, tag sales, estate sales, and pottery shows almost totally within the state of California, at prices ranging from one dollar to the high end of the spectrum.

Values in the price guide are on an average range, based on prices found in California. Prices for any given item may be higher or lower in a particular region and because of high or low demand. Condition and decoration, as well as demand, affect prices and cause them to vary. The value guide is meant only as a guide.

Buyer, beware! Very rare, one-of-a-kind or signed pieces will be marked NPA (no price available) since these are considered priceless. Also, with increased interest, prices have moved upward dramatically in the past few years and may well continue that trend. Please note, piece numbers and/or date introduced are given where available.

Introduction

At the turn of the twentieth century, many artists journeyed to California to live and work, happy to call this beautiful state their home. The warm climate brought people from around the world as well as across the country to find their golden dream in the entertainment industry and the arts. In the field of ceramic art, pottery became a major influence in Southern California. The state's close ties to Mexico, Central America, and the Asian countries exerted a strong influence on the function and design of many products made in the state.

Through the years, hundreds of ceramic studios and factories were established in California, from Oceanside to Pasadena and from Santa Barbara to San Marcos. Several of the factories, including Catalina, Bauer, Brayton, and Vernon Kiln, gained prominence through the use of quality materials and the production of outstanding pieces.

Purely functional items, such as pipes, were the ceramic pieces initially produced. Decorative tiles and dinnerware became popular with the public and later, figurines and other collectibles rounded out the selection.

As with most businesses of the era, these pottery plants were run by men with male chemists, designers and production foremen. Women generally were assigned the tasks of painting and decorating figures and dinnerware and little else. One of the women who broke this mold was Kay Finch.

Kay Finch was a pioneer in several ways for she was not only a member of a select group of female ceramic artists but also she was successful in almost every venture she ever undertook.

Exhibiting artistic flair at an early age, Kay was encouraged by family members and school teachers to develop this talent and because she created from her heart, she designed ceramics which the public took to its heart.

In every decade or so, there are creations that become symbols for happiness or good will. People feel happy looking at Mickey Mouse's face, the smiley face stickers, the pet rock, or today's collectible angels. Kay Finch pioneered in this genre with her round, flower-bedecked piggies that made World War II America smile.

Enter any gift shop today and you will find humorous collectibles—angels, animals, figures of charm and detail. Kay Finch pioneered in this field not only with her famous piggies but also with her little angels designed in 1937. These figures topped the best seller chart for two decades and further proved that the artist was a woman ahead of her time. Kay's creations have a true sense of whimsy in their design and execution but careful inspection will testify that these are works of art, true sculpture. The sense of style, color, proportion, and detail is unmatched and uniquely Kay Finch. From 1937 to 1963, Kay's studio and work may have changed and expanded but her commitment to quality always remained intact.

Even her later endeavors which included original designs in bronze, ceramics, and even cement, always displayed not only the sculptor's artistic talent but her strong sense of individuality.

Kay Finch ceramics command as much popularity with collectors today as they did when they were originally sold. People respond readily to the charm and happiness these creations embody as they perch on shelf or table. The decorative figures, bowls, and vases are beautiful, functional, and inspirational as the smiles they produce attest. Kay Finch always seemed able to capture the essence of each creation as well as its physical form. When seeking to identify Kay Finch figures, look at the eyes—their souls are in their eyes, liquid and shining.

Kay surrounded by her ceramic creations.

Production Marks

KF CALIF.

Earliest mark we have found.

KERAMICS KAY (vertical oval label)

Paper label 1939-1940.

KAY FINCH CORDNA DEL MAR

Early 1940s.

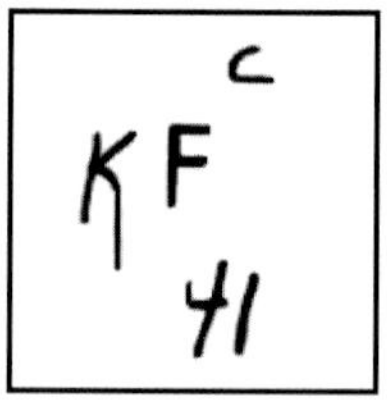

KF c 41

1941 mark.

KAY FINCH

Early 1950s. Stamped mark.

K. Finch Calif.

Early 1950s. Incised mark.

Kay Finch CALIFORNIA

Red stamp. Also found combined with previous mark.

Kay Finch CALIFORNIA

Back-stamp.

Kay Finch CALIFORNIA

Painted red, green or black. Found with mark #12.

BABY'S FIRST from CALIFORNIA to (circular)

Under-glaze. Early 1950s

Kay Finch CALIFORNIA

Very narrow green stamp imprint.

KAY FINCH CALIFORNIA

1950s mark. Found hand-lettered and/or glazed inside indented base.

FROM Kay and Braden

Signatures on personal gifts.

K Finch

Early 1940s. Inked mark.

Kay Finch

Original signature found.

Kay Finch

Stamped.

K Finch

1940s mark. Deeply incised.

Kay Finch CALIFORNIA (with crown)

Late 1950s – early 1960s. Gold paint.

Stamped mark. Found with and without waves.

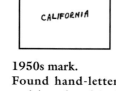

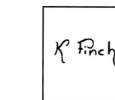

Kay Finch Calif

Late 1950s mark. Incised.

KAY FINCH CALIFORNIA

Late 1950s incised mark.

Kay Finch: Her Life and Art

Anyone can tell just by glancing at her creations that Kay Finch loved animals—pigs, dogs, cats, horses. Each and every subject was cast in charming pose and style, with great attention to detail. This love for animals began at age five with an announcement that she "didn't want to go to Heaven." Asked to explain, Kay declared, "Teacher says that horses and dogs don't go to Heaven, so I don't want to go either." From that moment and for the rest of her life, Kay devoted herself to all God's creatures through her creations.

Katherine Seamon Finch was born August 19, 1903, in Sunset Heights in El Paso, Texas. Her father, Frank H. Seamon, was a professor at Texas College of Mines while her mother stayed at home raising Kay and her brother and sister, Mayo and Mary Virginia. As most children do, Kay and her redheaded siblings liked to play, and often they sculpted in the mud in the vacant lot next to their home. On one occasion, young Kay disappeared with the family dictionary only to be found in an adobe brickyard several blocks away, sitting in the mud modeling a horse from a picture in the book. Kay would doodle all the time and had the tendency to bring home whatever stray animals she found so she could study their every move. Throughout her schooling in El Paso, her parents never deprived her of clay, art supplies or inspiration but little did anyone imagine that Kay would grow to become a world renowned master sculptress.

Kay began her formal art education after graduation from El Paso High School. In 1920, with strong encouragement from her family, she enrolled at Ward Belmont College in Nashville, Tennessee, later being admitted to the Memphis (Tennessee) Academy of Arts. While in college, Kay also turned her attention to the sport of tennis. She excelled, winning both singles and doubles championships in a tri-state competition among Tennessee, Mississippi, and Arkansas, and continued her winning ways in tournaments involving Arizona, New Mexico, and her home state of Texas.

Seven-year-old Kay with mother Katherine Seamon.

Kay, nine years old, on left, at friend's party.

It was in Memphis in 1922 that Kay met and fell in love at first sight with Braden L. Finch. A few months later, she married the man who would share her enthusiasms and projects for a lifetime. Braden was born in New York and moved with his family to Memphis. He was a cartoonist with sharp intelligence, a winning personality, and a strong belief in both his own abilities and his wife's talent. In 1929, searching for the California dream, the Finches moved to Santa Monica and in 1930 settled in a modest house on the beach in Ventura County north of Los Angeles. Braden landed a job at the local paper in the advertising department. Within three short years, he became editor of the *Santa Paula Chronicle*.

Kay devoted her time to raising their family of three children—Frances, George, and Cabell, and spent any spare time attending art class at the Santa Barbara School of Art, riding her horses, and teaching art at Saint Catherine's to local children. In addition, Kay also apprenticed at a ceramic studio in Santa Barbara with Andrew C. Simons. Simons had studied at the Pennsylvania Academy of Fine Arts and with Dampt and Rodin in Paris. The class that Kay studied was Life Modeling which included instruction in anatomical form and construction. Methods of plaster casting were also explained and illustrated. This is where Kay probably acquired her knowledge of mold making and casting.

In January 1935, Kay began modeling in cement a life-size statue of her youngest son Cabell in the form of a fountain. In April of that year, the piece was exhibited in Santa Barbara. Then in 1937 Braden was offered a job as editor of *The Santa Ana Journal*, the city's evening newspaper. The family moved into a Victorian home at 733 Flower Street in Santa Ana. Braden went to work, the kids went to school, and Kay continued to sculpt and work with clay.

Deciding to take further instruction, Kay enrolled at Scripps College in Claremont, where she received her most thoughtful and insightful training. Under the direction of William Manker, Kay was pushed to produce her best. "Mr. Manker made me keep re-sculpting the same horse over and over until I was so sick of that horse," she declared. Those first figures became known as the Manker horses. Manker was a California native who began his work in clay as a designer for Ernest Batchelder in 1924.

Manker then founded the ceramics department at Scripps College in 1934. He was able to pass on to students like Kay and Howard Pierce his own knowl-

The Manker horses.

edge and practical experience in pottery production and an understanding of the arts and crafts movement. Manker's encouragement soon led to bigger and better things. Kay's terra cotta sculptures so stirred her teacher that he urged her to pursue her art as a profession rather than a hobby. Shortly afterward, Kay sold models of a horse and a dog to Durlin Brayton of Brayton Laguna Pottery in Laguna Beach.

In any free time she had, Kay began to sculpt everything, including her saddle horse Smoky and some of her dogs "just for fun," and fire the pieces in the kilns at Claremont or Santa Ana College. The results were stupendous. Soon friends wanted duplicates to give as gifts and many other people also wanted to buy them. In June of 1937 Barker Brothers, a Los Angeles design and decorating store, heard of her work and ordered the figurines in large lots. Kay's first sale of angels to the store netted $8.00 which she unfortunately had to spend on a speeding ticket.

In February 1938, several of Kay's models, including the Manker horses, were sent to the Los Angeles County Museum for inclusion in a special pottery exhibition. Later that same year, the San Diego Museum exhibited her horse figurine, Equus. Increasing demand for her adorable figures of dogs, angels, and horses soon overburdened Kay's small home and work space.

In order to further her production, Kay purchased a second-hand Denver kiln for the princely sum of $35.00. That was a substantial outlay in the late depression year of 1938, but well worth the price. With this action, Kay Finch Ceramics was officially born in Southern California. In a small milk shed in the backyard dubbed Smokehouse Studio, production began with clay, plaster, pigments, and tools rounding out the initial inventory. The shed was lined with newspaper to keep out the elements and the printed comics on the wall also helped to pass the time when something exploded in the kiln. Soon Braden took the time to learn the ceramic trade of making molds by attending some classes with Kay and helped to make the first molds by lifting and carrying the heavy objects. With the kiln, Kay began turn-

Kay and son Cabell and the Smokehouse Studio, Santa Ana, 1938.

ing out creations that made her smile. They were in pink-tinted clay, of course, since that was one of her favorite colors.

In May of 1938, the Finches finally took a long awaited trip around the world. To Kay, the trip was much more than a mere get-away or a romantic time spent with her husband. In China, Japan, Arabia, France, Germany and all the other countries on this tour, Kay observed how art and design in ceramics were produced. This insight into other cultures led to dramatic inspirations in some of her own designs and dec-orating techniques. On their travels, Kay collected horses and dogs made in each country she visited. In Ara-bia especially, the artist wanted to

The Finches' passport photo, 1938.

get a representation of one of their famous Arabian horses. This proved impossible, for she found that their religion prohibits them from making an image of living things.

After the world trip, Kay took a job at the interior decorating firm of Ferne Irwins where she sold some of her little angels. The local newspaper art columnist saw her creations and encouraged Kay to continue to offer her work to other retail stores.

While involved in every aspect of the operations from concept to original sculpture to making molds, pouring, cleaning, decorating, kilning, and glazing, Kay took time to visit shop and store buyers throughout Southern California to show and sell her product. She was soon wearing out the soles of her shoes pounding the pavement for orders. On one of the early days of selling from samples, she did a staggering $60.00 worth of business. Soon, sales agents would take up her marketing chores which proved to be no hard job at all since the products really sold themselves. As the figurines had made their creator smile, so did they please the customers. Friends and the public alike were clamoring for the saucy little pigs and the winsome angels which the artist produced. Kay Finch was in business!

Seeing that the ceramic business was where they should direct their attention, Braden resigned from his position at the newspaper and began handling the business of the young company as general manager. With the continued increase in interest and demand, the Finches knew they had to expand.

Therefore in 1939, the Finches decided to purchase a two-lot parcel of land above an area called Buck Gulch with a small stucco house located at 3901 E. Pacific Coast Highway, then 121 Coast Highway, in the community of Corona del Mar. In August of that year a stu-dio/workroom was erected on the cliffs overlooking the Pacific Ocean. A small staff of three or four people was hired at this time to begin production but Kay and Braden did most of the work themselves. Every step in production took place in this one small room, from mold making to packing. They also built a residence for themselves on the west side of the proper-ty at 344 Hazel Drive.

First Corona del Mar one-room studio, 1939.

Birdseye view of Finch studio (1), residence (2), and site of new studio (3), with highway frontage marked, 1939.

Exterior of Finch residence, 344 Hazel Drive, Corona del Mar.

Interior view of living room.

While demand for her creations was increasing tenfold, Kay still remained very selective in what she produced. In 1940, Walt Disney Studio was searching for a company to create quality ceramic reproductions of characters from the new film *Fantasia*. Disney thought Kay's stylized pastel look would do justice to the film's figures, but Kay thought otherwise. As an artist, she wanted to produce her own original pieces, not copy someone else's work and vision. It was Vernon Kilns of Los Angeles who began producing the Fantasia ceramics in November of that year.

Within one year of its inauguration, the new building proved to be obsolete and another larger studio and showroom had to be constructed. So on December 7, 1941, Pearl Harbor Day, the new Kay Finch Ceramic Studio opened. This larger facility was built to meet the growing demand for the products. The 500-square-foot, 130-foot-long facility featured many connected rooms, including a full decorating department, tunnel kilns for increased production, a mold room, packing and shipping departments, and a sales shop for the curious drive-by public. The sage green and white building was designed by Frank Gruys of Beverly Hills, who also designed the Finch residence, and it fanned out in wings, hugging the ground. The building was constructed by local Balboa contractor Conrad Shook and employed new architectural techniques, including water resistant marine plywood and a roof made of crushed white ceramic tile. The timber support frame, concealed on the interior, but exposed on the exterior, made the building unique. This much-admired structure was the first with this type of architecture in California, having been introduced a few years earlier at the New York World's Fair. Outside, flowering plants and fruit trees surrounded a pool where Kay's sculpted Mer-baby relaxed in the seaside garden atmosphere.

New studio under construction, late summer, 1941.

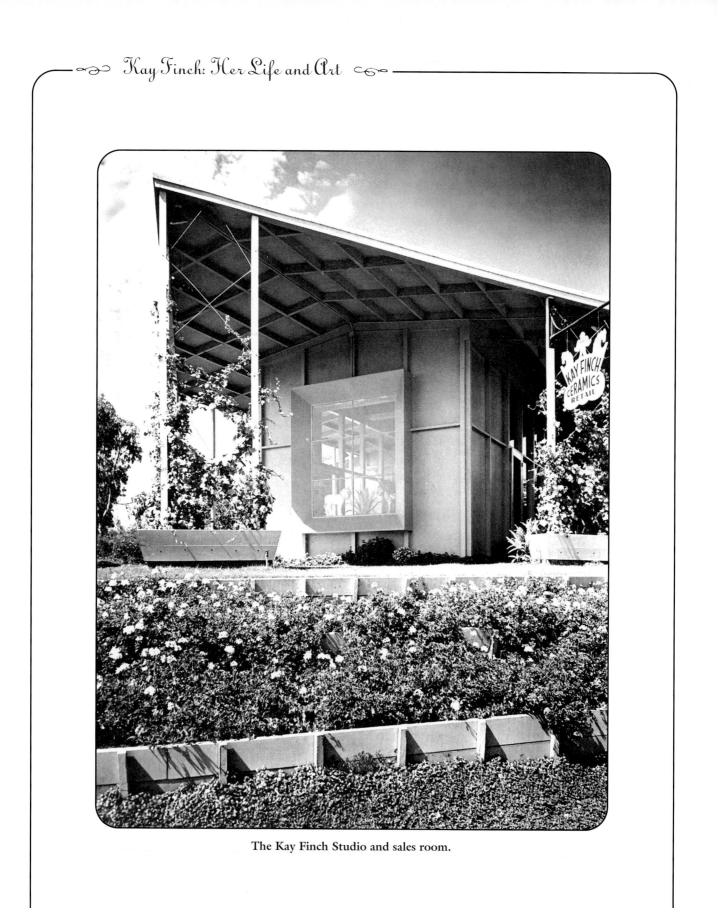

The Kay Finch Studio and sales room.

The new larger studio not only offered the Finches more space, but also better control of their ceramics operation. Kay continued to do all the sculpting in her private studio behind the new building but left the actual production of the ceramics to her talented staff. Her favorite subjects were, of course, animals and she drew inspiration from everyday life. "I like animals. They're sort of a hobby with me," she said as she sculpted what she liked. Trips to the circus and zoos and surrounding farms and stables led to the creations of horses, lambs, cats, dogs, rabbits, pigs, camels, elephants, penguins, chickens, owls, and many, many more. Kay's own Dalmatian, Judy, posed as the model for the Coach Dog and one of her personal favorites was a life-size lamb with a ring of hand-formed and hand-applied flowers around its neck.

Kay posing with her Dalmatian Judy, early 1940s.

Kay sculpting Pete Penguin, circa 1942.

Frank Seamon and Mayo Seamon, Kay's father and brother, admire sculpture of her dad.

People were also a popular subject with Kay. A peasant couple and a Scandinavian boy and girl were early favorites as were the elegantly detailed Victorian Godey couples in summer or winter apparel direct from the pages of Louis A. Godey's magazine. Kay's travels and studies of people and art around the world produced museum quality ceramic replicas of Asian court ladies and their lord, Chinese children, an American Indian family, South Seas women, and others. Angels and religious items were produced in abundance including several Madonnas, choir boys and a bride and groom wedding cake topper.

The pigs were perhaps the most successful figures. Grumpy, Smiley, and Sassy as well as the baby and the bitsy pigs were added to the line in 1940 and 1941. The large life-size pig, Grandpa, was also known as Gerry if decorated in geraniums and was introduced for Christmas 1940.

Kay with her Pottery Pig family.

Kay's sculpting style is unique in that her works project a sense of whimsy in their execution, while still being faithful to the physical realities of the subjects. Each and every piece has her one-of-a-kind trademark style in its design implementation but close inspection will attest that these sculptures are always anatomically correct and in perfect proportion. The artist made sure each pose of every animal and human figure had the proper and natural distribution of weight applied to the sculptures. Kay collected and drew inspiration from many famous artists, including Michelangelo. One of her top favorites was children's book illustrator Dorothy Lathrop whose books she collected. The authors have a book on Brueghel which belonged to Kay. She supported many artists by patronizing gallery openings and made friends with other area artists by attending events and purchasing their artwork as gifts or to add to her own collection. Claremont artist Jean Goodwin and Kay became fast friends, attending art classes together at the University of Southern California. Kay collected many of her friend's sculptures and was even captured in oils by the artist. Kay and Braden also enjoyed going to the theater and movies and fast became part of the coastal community's social set, attending many functions and parties. These facts are further proof that Kay cared deeply about her work and community. She was a master artist and a very involved person.

Every step of production was done in this one room from mid 1939 to late 1941.

Kay and Braden pose with growing staff, fall 1939.

Studio staff, 1941. First row, fourth and fifth from left: Kay with sister, Mary Virginia Seamon Schultz. Top row, second from right: Kay's father, professor Franklin H. Seamon.

World War II hit hard and fast in the United States and all too soon after the opening of the Finch studio. The government put bans on thousands of products and materials that were deemed essential for fighting and winning the war. Many businesses had to change gears and actually start producing gears for machines and other war-related items. Fortunately for Kay and Braden, wartime was their boom time and they could continue to receive non-essential materials for producing their ceramics. Since the war had cut off trade with Asian and European countries, the many department and specialty stores across the U.S. clamored for products to fill their shelves. Before World War II, 95 percent of the world's ceramics were made in Europe and Asia but during the war years, American ceramic companies numbering close to 600 dominated the market and filled the gap.

Kay Finch Ceramics entered the national distribution market by displaying their wares at the Ruth Sloan Shops in Los Angeles, Robert P. Pierce in Chicago, M. Wille Art Goods in New York, and through their own catalogs. Ads for Finch ceramics would also be found in national magazines such as *Sunset* and *The New Yorker*. Store buyers from across the country began purchasing Finch products for their own shops. Because of their fine reputation for quality and price, Kay Finch Ceramics sold in only the best stores including Bullock's Wilshire in Los Angeles, City of Paris and Gumps in San Francisco, Marshall Fields in Chicago, Nieman-Marcus in Dallas and Saks Fifth Avenue in New York City. By the mid-decade, Kay's work could be seen and bought in over 1,500 retail outlets in the United States alone. In the 1940s Kay Finch Ceramics joined the ranks with I. Magnin and a select few prestigious California companies to open a boutique in the exclusive Hotel del Coronado in San Diego.

Ruth Sloan showroom, Chicago, mid 1940s.

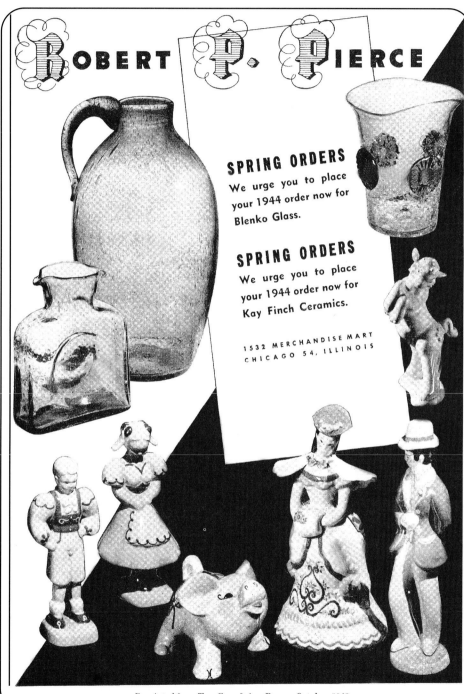

Reprinted from THE GIFT & ART BUYER, *October, 1943*

Advertisement to remind retailers to place their orders for 1944.

NEIMAN-MARCUS
Dallas 1, Texas

July 8, 1944

Mrs. Kay Finch
Corono del Mar,
California

My dear Mrs. Finch:

This is a note to tell you that it was such a pleasure to meet
you and your husband and to see your very interesting studio.
It has given me great inspiration and I fully appreciate, more
than ever, the lovely work you are doing.

I only wish our Department were larger so that I definitely could
feature more of your things than I do, but our space is very
limited and it seems impossible to get a large enough space
for your lovely things.

I could very definitely feel the spirit you have instilled in
your factory as soon as I walked through it. I think it is a
great accomplishment to do lovely creative work and then be
able to produce it.

My very kindest regards to you and Mr. Finch and assuring
you the visit with you was one of the bright spots of my
California trip, I am

Very sincerely yours,

Cay Vedder, Buyer
Decorative Galleries

CV:sf

Letter from Dallas's famed Neiman-Marcus,
1944.

J. W. ROBINSON CO. *Seventh Street & Grand Avenue • Mutual 0333 • Los Angeles*

December 24, 1943

Kay Finch Ceramics
121 Coast Highway
Corona Del Mar, Calif.

Gentlemen:

To you and to all the personnel of your firm
we wish as happy a New Year as is possible
under the present circumstances.

But even as with this greeting we look forward to the year that is coming, we must
look back over the year that is just com-
pleted. In both directions we feel that
there is much that is gratifying.

For we have greatly appreciated your fine
friendliness and your willing and gracious
cooperation. There have been difficulties
for us all, in the nation and in the business world. But such understanding and
service as yours have helped us to attain
a fine degree of success.

We therefore look toward a continuation of
our association. And may 1944 bring peace
again to the world, security to our nation
and a furtherance of the mutual good will
of your firm and ours.

Very truly yours,

W. W. Kirk
Vice-President

WWK:W

Letter from Los Angeles-based J.W. Robinson
Company, Christmas, 1944.

Kay's figures soon became so popular that her family and friends were trying to identify her creations in magazine spreads like *Better Homes and Gardens* and on motion picture sets. With war's end, trade opened up as fast as it had shut down and Kay's ceramics entered the foreign market then being made available in 21 countries, including Mexico and Cuba, and in Central America, Australia, and South Africa. With all this activity, Kay Finch Ceramics reached its peak with close to 65 employees in 1945.

Robinson's Department Store uses Finch Studio sales room for ad background.

In the mid 1940s, Kay began making larger pieces in limited production because the artist decided to "go for originals more than mass production." One of the first of these pieces was the Cathay or Chinese Princess, standing a little over three feet tall. Only ten decorated ones were produced, each different from the other, but all finished and decorated by hand. These sculptures originally sold for $750.00, which was a high price for that time. Several bisque Chinese Princesses were produced for garden sculptures and head busts can also be found. A smaller 23" Chinese Princess was also produced but it is not as elaborately detailed as the larger one. Other larger art figures followed, including the Tang Horse or Stallion, Petey the Donkey, Madonna Holding Babe and Violet the Elephant.

Life-sized Lamb, #167. 20".

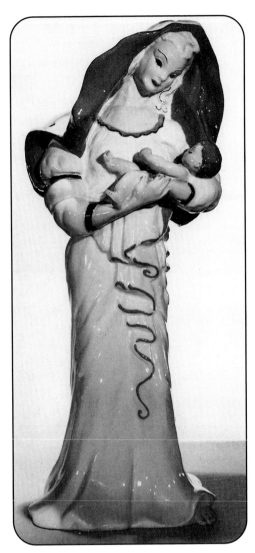

Madonna, #4858. 16".

Petey the Donkey display at Laguna Beach Festival of the Arts, 1947.

Since ceramic work was the rage in the 1940s, many from Los Angeles on their way to and from Laguna Beach would stop by the studio to meet and talk with Kay and buy a memento or two to take home. Kay had done some commission work in her schooling years and continued to do others when she had the time. She designed dinnerware for dance guru Arthur Murray and produced special figures for several interior designers. She also designed garden and fountain sculptures and reliefs and displays for the Orange County Fair in Anaheim in 1948 and the famous Art Festival in Laguna in 1947-50.

Sea Baby, unfinished pink terra cotta. Sculpted for studio fountain, 1941.

KAY FINCH CERAMICS

HOW THEY GROW

Kay Finch Studios, Corona del Mar, Calif.

The moment you see one of Kay Finch's loveable ceramic creations you want to touch it . . . . to draw it closer. You begin to live with it as though it already belonged to you. A rare quality to find in any work, but immeasurably greater because of its rarity.

Kay Finch is as American as the wide stretches of Texas where she was born. Her artistic conceptions are completely American . . . young . . . vital . . . growing from American background . . . freedom . . . originality and democratic direction.

Kay started sculpturing in clay when she was just a babe. An art student later in the South, and a traveler in Europe and the Orient, she drew inspiration from every experience. She can turn her hand to any subject. Prim Godey couples right out of the family album . . . coquettish peasants dressed for a light opera chorus . . . and gay little animals that make you smile with pleasure.

Who-oo — but Kay Finch would have created these three solemn little Owls . . . so wise . . . so amusing and so charming . . . that you'll never tire of them?

Kay Finch's work combines fine modeling . . . a sure knowledge of glaze and color with punctillious attention to detail, which means thorough-going quality throughout. Every piece is free hand painted . . . often enchantingly flower decorated and featuring somehow, somewhere, her individual and lovely pinks, rich greens and pastels. Kay Finch Ceramics blend with complete harmony into modern or period interiors . . . quick to become a harmonious part of any home, office, studio or salon.

Among the hundreds of fascinating ceramic personalities Kay Finch creates, there is not one note of somberness or the grotesque. Rather you see a family of loveable little masterpieces which delight at first glance and become treasured possessions as time goes by. Kittens, Dogs, Chickens, each with infinite charm and attraction. A fat Hippopotamus with a purple bow . . . little Indians and prancing Horses that fairly quiver with life. Gleaming Fish and Shells to round out a beautiful ceramic family far too numerous to list.

Loveable Piglettes . . . modeled in gaily flower patterned mood with a touch of undeniable whimsy . . . that stamps them instantly as Kay Finch pieces.

Finch Catalog, 1944.

With the success of the studio, the Finches were soon able to purchase 160 acres near the picturesque small town of Julian, set high in the mountains overlooking San Diego. It was here amongst the pine and oak trees that Kay and Braden relaxed. The valleys and fields were covered with wild briar roses and Kay decided to make a set of dinnerware, featuring these beautiful flowers, for the small, rose-covered ranch house on the property. A year or so later, the Briar Rose design was adapted into full-scale production pieces at the studio. Blue Daisies and, in 1947, a pattern called California Calico were added. Unfortunately, these hand-produced quality place settings were made only for a few years.

Breakfast sets introduced in summer, 1946. Briar Rose pattern shown.

"CORRAL"
Open stock pattern.
Heavy white glaze with
hand painted designs
in tan, chartreuse and
green.

CORRAL OR CALICO DINNEDWARE	
4634 Plate 10½"	1.50
4750 Plate 9½"	1.25
4726 Plate 7¾"	1.00
4757 Plate 6¾"	.90
4751C Cup, Saucer	1.25
4755 Creamer	1.10
4734 Covered Sugar	1.40
4759 Jam Jar, Spoon	1.50
4728 Tea Tile	1.00
4753 Cereal Bowl	1.00
4814 Serving Bowl 6"	1.20
4752 Serving Bowl 7"	1.50
4810 Serving Bowl 9"	1.60
4821 Serving Bowl 11"	3.75
4820 Platter	2.50
4756 Shakers, each	.50

Corral Dinnerware inspired by Kay's love for horses, 1947.

California Calico Dinnerware, 1947.

Buffet ware, hand-decorated with hens and roosters, 1947.

While Kay created the art work, Braden remained the backbone of the operations. His business management skills as a newspaper editor for so many years were invaluable in the handling of the sixty some employees of the studio. Braden was a people person and had a wonderful personality and spirit, working well with everyone and pitching in with whatever needed to be done when the work schedule was tight. Braden and Kay became fast learners in the technical side of ceramics production. In the beginning they thought they could handle the jobs of mold making, drying, kilning, and other areas, but soon found that they needed to hire several professionals for these positions.

Braden also kept busy with politics. He was a member of the Newport Beach City Council for several years and also was a member of the local school board, parks commission, and president of the Newport Beach and Corona del Mar Chambers of Commerce. Braden was also an active environmentalist and spearheaded the drives to purchase natural coastline along Corona del Mar for public parks and the program for the clean-up and protection of Newport's beaches and tide pools. Many of his programs are on-going, thanks to his energy and foresight.

more effective <u>longer</u>!

Now contains amazing new ingredient M-3 — that protects against odor-causing bacteria

New **MUM**
cream deodorant

Product of Bristol-Myers

Mum advertisement with Finch ceramics around mirror, 1940s.

The major outlets for introducing new ceramics were the popular gift-ware shows held each year across the country. Kay would generally present about two dozen designs annually and many of these designs were the highlights of these shows. Store buyers would eagerly await her latest sculptures. Kay Finch Ceramics was one of only a handful of companies that received more reorders for their existing products along with the newly introduced ones because of their quality and high sales. Sales agents would report back to the studio on what were hot sellers. The 1945 bestseller list included all the pigs, the Godeys, the owls, the farmyard Biddy hen and Butch rooster, the angels, and many others. At these shows, Kay became acquainted with other famous California ceramic artists of the day, including Hedi Schoop and Sascha Brastoff.

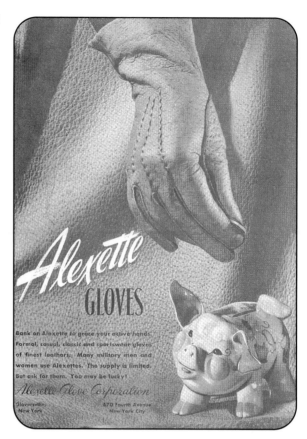

Glove ad features Smiley Pig in *Mademoiselle* magazine, January, 1944.

Sunset ad, January, 1944.

New Yorker ad, February, 1944.

Dealer Robert P. Pierce announces that retailers could order Finch Ceramics for fall, 1944.

We are happy to announce that Kay Finch is accepting orders for Fall!

Visit our Showrooms during the coming market and place your Kay Finch order for fall delivery (we do regret that new accounts cannot be accepted). See also our other lines on display ★ Beautiful Magic in Glass paper weights ★ Sculptured Wood figures and wall pieces in authentic Chinese motifs ★ L'Atelier Chic sudsable boudoir accessories ★ Antiques of every description, Porcelains, Silver, Copper, Brass, hundreds of interesting and unusual pieces.

ROBERT P. PIERCE
1532 MERCHANDISE MART, CHICAGO 54, ILL.

Court Ladies spring up as table centerpieces, 1944.

Ad for ceramic Yorkshires, December, 1945.

From *Giftwares*, February, 1946.

Kay believed in variety in her ceramics line. She produced large 36" figures as well as small 1" ones with prices ranging from 50 cents to over $700.00. The figures tended to be expensive but they were produced in the best possible way and with the best materials. With Kay as the sole designer of the studio, the line was uniform in respect to a style and design not achieved at other ceramic companies where several designers would produce objects and sculptures for the line.

Kay, Braden, and the rest of the staff took great pride in the fact that they never copied the designs of other artists. All of the designs, colors, and glazes produced by the company were exclusively Finch. Kay strongly felt that, "Everyone should develop his own style and individuality and try to reach the highest standard possible." Concerning the practice of repeating and imitating what had already been done, Kay states, "Those who copy the designs of others, even though their work may be beautiful, are making a grave mistake. What I know I learned from someone else. But I express it differently. I like to share my ideas and help others. Sharing of ideas stimulates competition and enriches the culture of the world." These were words she truly lived.

Kay would take her time in the development of a sculpture. She always kept a scrapbook where she would sketch a subject repeatedly until she was completely satisfied with it. Then in her private studio, Kay would develop the figure in three dimensions, often

Large Rabbit, #4622.

reworking it to get the piece exactly the way she wanted. She also did many watercolor sketches on decoration of the finished piece or what variations in color and designs would be included in the line. To keep the figures authentic, Kay had to be knowledgeable on everything from fur patterns on animals to the shape, size, and colors of California flowers to ethnic costumes. Vast volumes of art and numerous reference books were kept for her research and information needs.

Kay's brother-in-law, Alfred Schultz, was a chemist who helped to produce the special clay, glazes, and colors that the studio used. Unusual and vibrant hues were developed and this proved to be one of the reasons that no other firm came close to the quality and originality of Finch Ceramics.

Original watercolor sketches by Kay Finch with paint names listed for decorators.

Sketch of Kay's Dalmatian Judy, 1942.

Kay loved animals and always had them around her. The ceramic cat Ambrosia was known as Princess Pushkin in the Finch household, known also as the Russian Rat Killer. The Finches sheltered birds, a goat, and many other animals as well. Most of the time Kay would model an animal and it would stay on as a new family member. Dogs were her favorite, especially one breed. "I like my Yorky terriers. I try to model them with life," Kay declared about modeling her little friends. This love of dogs grew as the pottery grew and eventually became a successful venture in its own right.

In the early 1940s Kay began a second hobby/business, Crown Crest Kennels. Dog breeding was not new to Kay. In El Paso, pet Chihuahuas were very popular for breeding but it was in Memphis that the artist began breeding more seriously. To Kay, Yorkshire Terriers were very glamorous and the perfect show dog to spotlight the best that she could breed. She became very prominent in this field and one of the first of a few who raised and bred champion terriers and Afghan hounds (the oldest purebred dogs in the canine world) in her kennels in the gully next to the studio. Kay's greatest champion was Taejon (known as Jonny to his friends) who won best in show in his breed in 19 competitions and was shown all over the United States.

Kay with her champion Afghans.

Ceramic Afghans guard
Crown Crest sign.

Kay's champion wins another award.

Kay and her friend Ruby Buchanan Jordan would exhibit their Afghans at shows up and down the state of California. "We would load the dogs in the back of Kay's stationwagon and off we'd go. It was a lot of work but also a lot of fun," remembers Ruby. Kay and her dogs won many awards and she would often give a ceramic dog trophy or personalized figurine to the owners of the winning dog. She was a member of the Afghan Hound Club of America and a patron of the Afghan Hound Club of New South Wales, Australia.

Crown Crest could accommodate about thirty dogs and most of them were bred to be champions, including several generations of Toy York champions. Kay again traveled the country and would show and judge dog shows, including the prestigious Westminster Show in New York City's famed Madison Square Garden. Crown Crest became world renowned for its top breeding and the importing and exporting of fine canines.

Kay's love for her dogs led to further inspiration in her ceramics. Throughout the 1950s she began introducing vast amounts of dog sculptures modeled on best in show winners. Rudiki was one of Kay's favorite creatures both as Afghan Hound and also as one of the first art pieces produced in both bronze and ceramic in a tribute to her friend Marion Florshine, the Grand Dame of Afghan Hounds.

The twelve American Kennel Club Champions which Kay reproduced in ceramic included the Cocker Spaniel, Poodle, Airedale, Scotty, Boxer, Pomeranian, Dachshund, Westie, Bull Malteje, Yorky, and Afghan. These beautiful ceramics were produced in their natural colors as opposed to the pink and pastel slip decoration of the 1940s.

Original terra cotta wall plaque by Kay.

Three little Afghan angels, #4911, #4963 and #4964.

Afghan art in Kay's living room.

The company itself continued to prosper with the addition of new ceramics. By 1947, the studio posted $150,000.00 in revenues. Other canine ceramics were added to the line over the years, including trophies, banks, ash trays, wall plaques, steins, and jewelry. These items could be special ordered to include hand decoration, lettering and gold and silver glazing. A grand surprise occurred in 1948 when a representative of President Harry S. Truman ordered specially decorated Southern Comfort Missouri Mule mugs from the studio for his re-election campaign. It was a good year for Truman and an excellent one for the Finches.

By 1950, changes were occurring rapidly in giftware operations within the United States. Trade agreements had been re-established with many foreign countries after the war and the imports were again flooding the market. The European and Asian communities could create dinnerware and decorative items far less costly than the ones being produced in the states. Lower production costs and salaries abroad along with larger factories brought stiff competition to the home front. Many domestic operations had to begin adapting and reducing overhead or else start closing their doors.

The Finches make a toast to their success with Truman's Missouri Mule mugs, 1948.

Among these new imports came many copies of the Finch ceramics. On this Kay said, "I do not believe in direct imitation of one artist by another. Art needs originality, much more of it. So while I am willing to tell everything I know about it, I have always refused to let any other potter make exact copies of my work." Unfortunately Kay and her company had to deal with a mass onslaught of unauthorized ceramics.

Leaf pattern planters introduced in 1952, #5220-1.

18", Wall plaques, #5820 and #5821, and assorted Ming vases.

Flower arranger bowls.

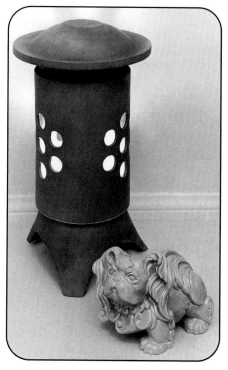

Foo Dog, #5601, with giant garden lantern, #5578.

Moon vases: smallest to largest, #5646, #5645, #5967, #5503 and #5502.

Because of the high quality of Kay's ceramics, the Finch operation was affected little in production output but the company made many changes in order to stay in a game so altered by added competition and changing consumer buying patterns. Braden felt that by increasing the product output and gearing toward certain specialized trade lines, the company would increase growth. In the 1950s new lines were introduced, including Baby's First from California featuring pink, blue, and yellow blocks, books, and planters with rabbits, bears, kittens, puppies, lambs, and babies attached. Holiday ceramics were increased in the line including turkeys for Thanksgiving, and bunnies, chicks, and eggs for Easter. Christmas inspired a vast variety of items including nativity sets, angels, planters, and a Santa Claus line featuring mugs, wall pockets, punch bowls, cookie jars, sack holders, and large charger plates. In 1950 the operation was one of the first American companies to promote annual Christmas plates, producing one for each year until 1962. A 1962 plate exists, but it was probably never put into full production.

Another change occurred in the decorating department, see next chapter. Throughout the 1940s most of the ceramics were fully hand decorated with colored slips, a thinned liquid clay, then scraffito etching detail was done on the slip. This decorating process was time consuming and expensive. Consumer trends in decorating were also leaning away from the cartoon color slip painting of the past decade. The return of the 1930s' lusters or pink pearl glazes came in around 1950. Colors of this glossy, opalescent paint included clear pearl, pink, ruby red, and green. Gold detailing over glaze was also very popular.

Easter eggs and bunnies.

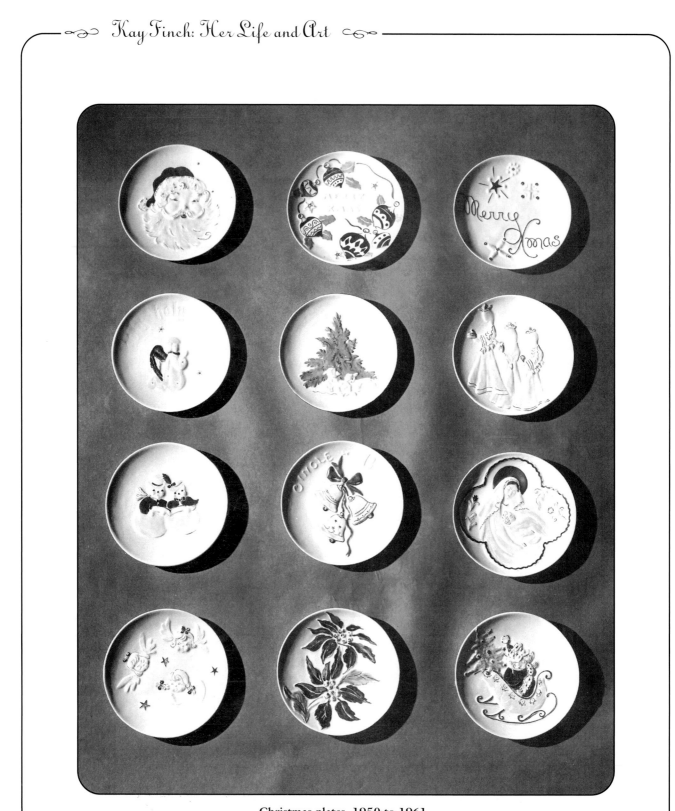

Christmas plates, 1950 to 1961.

Reindeer, #5475 and Sleigh, #5479.

Kay and the decorating department also experimented with other painting and glazing methods, including the beautifully airbrushed Siamese cat Anna and her lifelike three kittens and the champion dog line done in natural coloring. A high glaze, cocoa color which Kay dubbed Tanbark was also popular at this time. By 1953 most of the decorating girls were gone and only a few remained to do the limited detailing on some of the figures since most of the ceramics were now produced in solid colors.

Kay continued to sculpt all of the figures for the company but she could only do so much. Her son George had always had an interest in the operation and followed in his mother's footsteps by creating unique bowls and vases as well as many one-of-a-kind sculptures. George's work was quite different from his mother's, but the two complemented each other. Most of George's work was produced in solid colors in high glazes or matte finishes. Some of Kay's figures were then produced in a matching color to coordinate with the bowls and vases. Each year a new color and glaze would be introduced to the line. George's work is considered architectural in design and includes flower arranger bowls, petal bowls, and the peerless Ming bowls. The frogless Tops bowls were also popular when they were introduced into the line in 1959.

In the late 1950s the Talisman California line was introduced and marketed separately from the Finch line. These ceramic pieces included decorative table centerpieces, fruit bowls, and figures, all produced by George Finch.

Kay and George went on to create other ceramic items including bathroom wall plaques and lotion containers as well as kitchen canisters. Large ceramic fountains became popular around 1960. Especially in Southern California, new homes had large atriums for plants and decorative pool fountains. Beautifully detailed seahorses, sea nymphs, and mermaids supported by large shells and basins designed by the studio created exceptionally decorative and functional fountains.

Seahorse Fountain, 1960, #6063 and #6061.

Sea Nymph Fountain, #6064.

Because of Kay's reputation for ceramic quality, many, many copies can be found in the market place today. Most of her ceramics are marked; however, some are not. Close inspection will reveal the Finch quality in the ceramic base, painting decoration, glazing, and the clean mold lines. Ceramic factories both foreign and domestic copied and produced their own versions of Kay's originals, for whatever sells well will always be copied in ceramics. Copying is the sincerest form of flattery—and making a profit. Also hobbyists and crafts people produced their own molds from ceramics, etc.

The beginning of the end of Kay Finch Ceramics came when Braden Finch became ill in the autumn of 1961. Braden was hospitalized in December and passed away of myeloma on January 4, 1962. His dying wish was to keep the studio going, but Kay, nearing sixty, didn't know the financial end of the business as well as her husband and was also very busy with Crown Crest. Actual ceramic production ceased in the winter of 1962 and the close-out sale began in December 1962. On Saturday, March 23, 1963, Kay reluctantly closed her 24-year business for good.

Throughout her career, Kay had sculpted well over 700 individual designs for her company from 1937 to late 1961. That amount of quality work from one person is a staggering achievement. The encouragement and support from Braden, her children, family, friends, and a wonderful staff produced a quality American collectible that will live from generation to generation.

Studio garden, 1942. Chinese Princesses in terra cotta grace foreground.

With the close of the business, Kay devoted most of her time to her dogs, show judging, trips, and Crown Crest Kennels. In the early 1960s, Kay wrote many articles on dogs and judging for magazines including the local *Orange County Illustrated*. In 1971, Kay was asked by the Corona del Mar Chamber of Commerce to sculpt a memorial to her late husband Braden. Kay produced a sculpture of a mother sea lion and her pup that was cast into an 800 pound bronze statue. This was a fitting tribute to a man who spent his lifetime in the harbor area working for the preservation of beaches and tide pools, an undertaking continuing to this day. The memorial statue was placed in a natural grotto in a cluster of rocks at Inspiration Point next to Big Corona Beach, the same place Kay and Braden had seen live seals playing and resting years earlier. The 5' x 3' foot sculpture was lowered by helicopter to its home in the rocky island outcropping where today it is still visible from the cliffs above.

Kay with sea lion tribute to her late husband, 1971.

Plaque with tribute to Braden Finch.

SEA LIONS ON THE ROCK
BELOW ARE IN MEMORY OF
BRADEN FINCH – 1903-1962
FOR HIS YEARS OF DEDICATED
SERVICE TO OUR COMMUNITY
AND TO THE PRESERVATION
OF THIS COAST LINE.

Kay's bronze sea lion tribute to Braden nestled in its rocky home at Inspiration Point, Big Corona Beach.

In 1963 Freeman McFarlin's El Monte factory purchased some of Kay's designs and began producing the owls, chickens, and others in their own standard glazes and finishes. In the mid 1960s, Kay returned to produce original sculpture for Freeman McFarlin Potters in their San Marcos, California plant. The company also commissioned Kay on a royalty basis to produce new figures of dogs, cats, birds, and others. The association lasted about fifteen years until 1980. (See pp. 92 – 96). Kay had not lost her touch, for the figures are beautifully detailed and are found in solid colors, including gold with limited detailing. After her work for Freeman McFarlin, Kay decided to retire for good.

The original studio was leased out and spawned several different business ventures including an architect's office, a cosmetic shop, a church, and several restaurants over its final three decades. In 1993 the building was finally demolished. Kay Finch herself passed away on June 21, 1993, at the age of 89 in the city of Mountain View, California, near the home of her daughter, Frances Finch Webb.

It was the end of an era in the history of Orange County's California art pottery movement. It's true that the Finch studio flourished during a golden age of California pottery but the strength of her work won't permit that era to die. The legacy continues.

Kitten and Puppy baby dish and cup sets, #4856.

Elephant, #4845, and Donkey, #4846, ashtrays and cigarette holder, #4766.

Ashtrays in shells, flowers and leaves, clockwise from top left, #510, #4729, #4731, and #4730.

Packaged baby potty with pink or blue decoration and flower arrangement, #B-107.

Baby mug and cereal bowl, #506.

Cache pots, #505, #504, and #479.

Cute Dicky Birds in two poses, #4905.

The Studio in the 1940s

In 1941, the Kay Finch Studio had many production departments and many employees to fill available positions. Beginning with just four workers, the studio work force peaked in the mid and late 1940s with a crew of sixty-five. Studio employees were a close-knit family with everyone on a first name basis, including Kay and Braden. The staff often socialized after work hours at dances and parties. Hiring locally, Braden would recruit senior art students from Newport Harbor High School or place ads in the local newspaper. The students generally needed some art background and when hired, they were trained in departments ranging from mold pouring, trimming, and kilning to decorating. During the war years many of the workers were the wives and girlfriends of servicemen. These women took employment at the studio for the wages, the friendships, and the chance to pass the time doing useful work during this difficult era.

The war had cut off trade imports and many materials, including the precious metals that were used in war-related items, were difficult to find. Since fine gifts including wedding presents made of copper, silver and brass were impossible to obtain, pottery, especially ceramic pieces by Kay Finch and other firms, had become more popular than ever. The 1940s was truly the golden era for the ceramic studio.

The Finch studio itself was a one-story unit that featured many levels due to the natural banking of the landscape. The sales shop was in front close to Pacific Coast Highway with the decorating department a few steps behind. Braden and secretary Jessie Hill's offices overlooked the decorating girls' area. The facility was never called a factory, but was always known as a studio where everyone knew each other and all got along well. The beautiful gardens with reflection pools and sculptures

Jessie Hill, Braden's secretary for over 20 years.

and the intimate size of the building were all elements that lent themselves strongly to the name "studio" where art and beauty were created on a daily basis.

The production process at the studio was long and involved much human talent. Fortunately the facility was laid out in an organized manner through a progression of corridors and rooms that helped productivity in each step. At its peak, the Kay Finch studio produced about 150 finished figurines a day. Stan Skee was the principal mold maker for the studio in the 1940s and 1950s. If as the song says, "a good man is hard to find," then a good mold maker was even harder to find and keep. Many times other ceramic companies would try to lure away such a talented person to their own operation. Stan came from a potter's family in England and the ceramics trade was passed from his father to him with pride.

Skee's special talents were in such demand that he worked on freelance contract for Brayton Laguna Pottery in Laguna Beach, and Metlox Potteries in Manhattan Beach and later in his own studio. But it was at the Finches' that Stan enjoyed his job the most. "The studio was like family, everyone enjoyed each other and you took pride in the work you produced," Stan remembers.

The mold maker's job is the most essential part of ceramics production because it allows quality mass reproduction of an original piece of sculpture. The process itself moved in an orderly fashion. When Kay had finished perfecting a sculpture in modeling clay, it was given to Stan for his evaluation of the complexity of the piece. He would decide where the break undercuts and mold lines would lie, including how many parts of the block mold would be needed to reproduce the sculpture accurately.

Kay sculpts Smiley Pig, 1940.

While most block molds generally consist of two parts, Kay's creations almost always needed four, five or more parts. In a wooden box about 6 to 8 inches larger than the sculpture's perimeters, sections would be divided off with clay, then plaster would be poured into each section. Upon hardening, the sections would be pulled away, revealing a relief impression of part of the sculpture. When all the pieces were put together, the interior cavity formed a perfect indentation of the original sculpture. A master mold case is also made so that more production molds can later be made. Stan Skee was one of only a handful of skilled mold makers who could produce master molds for mass production of ceramic sculptures. With continued reuse of a mold, details become less defined due to the fine areas of the mold filling with clay residue. The details can be lost if the mold is used too many times. Molds could be reused only about 75 times before they had to be replaced with the worn-out molds being broken and destroyed to prevent reuse. The mold making process itself took one to three days to complete. (See pp. 62 – 63.)

In making the mold, unfortunately, the original sculpture was destroyed because the soft modeling clay tended to pull off the plaster as it was removed.

Many collectors have noticed that the pink tinted clay used on most of the 1940s pieces tends to be soft and therefore breaks and damages easily. It must be understood that the clay used was liquid and pliable to begin with so the artists could work on the figures, and as with any fine art, these delicate ceramics were meant to be displayed and not continually handled.

Mold cases line the new mold room, 1941.

Glaze cracking and crazing are evident on many pieces produced up until 1947. Even though the finest materials and production processes were employed in the creation of the ceramics, there are several rea-

sons these problems occurred. If the silica glaze ingredients were not mixed correctly, the glaze could shrink on the pottery's surface, producing a network of fine cracks (found on some early milky glazed 1937 - 42 pieces); pieces fired too quickly or too long; colder cooling temperatures outside the kiln; and the natural aging of the ceramics due to handling, extreme cold, heat, moisture, and sunlight also played parts.

Kay sculpts German Shepherd bust.

Even though many pre-1947 uncrazed pieces have been found, the studio remedied its problem and ceramics produced after that year have little or no crazing.

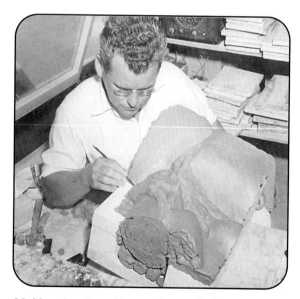

Mold maker Stan Skee sections off areas with clay to make mold of the German Shepherd bust.

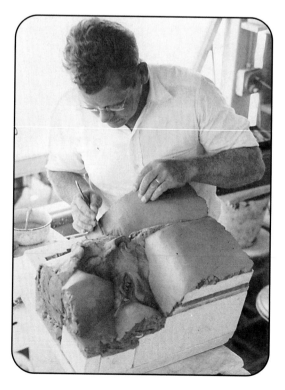

Mixing plaster.

Plaster is poured into section of mold.

15", Shepherd bust, "Grail", #478. This piece was done by Kay and is incised "Kay 1949." *$1,000.00 – 1,500.00*

Jesus Godines pours slip into mold at studio, 1941.

Grumpy Pig is carefully removed from mold, 1941.

Braden gets Smiley ready for his first firing.

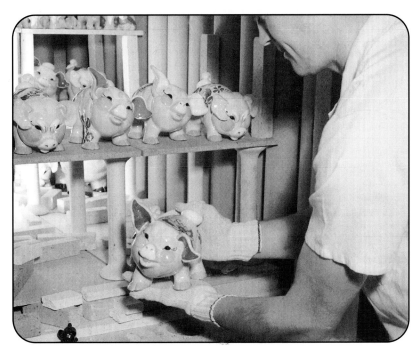

Smiley finally greets the world.

Raw materials for the production of these fine ceramics included top grade clays from Kentucky and Tennessee. These durable clays were finely ground in mills and mixed with water and talc from the California desert. Talc gave the clay a more pliable consistency. A coloring oxide tint was added to achieve the pink pastel hue of the clay. White and later yellow-tinted clays were also used. The thick, liquid clay would be mixed continuously to remove impurities and air bubbles. After the model was made and cleaned, it would be cast by being turned upside down and pressure clamped simultaneously with heavy-duty rubber straps to hold the parts together. The blocks would be placed in a large basin and the liquid clay would be poured from tubs and later overhead tubes, into the opening, actually the base of the figure, filling the mold to the rim.

The clay was allowed to thicken anywhere from 30 minutes to an hour depending on the size and complexity of the figure. Then a round hole was cut in the base and the block mold was flipped over and excess clay poured out through the hole for reuse. Workers had to be careful removing the mold pieces so as not to tear apart the delicate, moist figure. Some ceramic pieces that collectors find which are heavy and thick may have been left in the mold too long. Most ceramics that were too thick and heavy generally were destroyed. However, some figures were purposely allowed to jell to a heavy thickness so that extended parts would not break in shipping, the long-tailed pheasant being one of these examples.

Bisque ware waiting for next step in production.

The large Petey the Donkey figure, standing 30", had a block mold alone so complex and heavy that a special small crane was constructed to turn the immense mold over so that it could be filled with clay. In the production of ceramics, the finished pieces tend to shrink about 7 percent from the original sculpture size. In the case of Petey, such shrinkage would be scarcely noticeable. Issy Hiner and Lutie Belle Williamson Lindeman worked in the clay trimming and cleaning department, which was probably the messiest part of the studio. "Clay would get all over your clothes and by the end of the day, your apron turned hard and pink," states Lutie. After the figures were removed from their molds, they were still moist and were considered to be "plastic," still pliable and ready to be cleaned.

The trimmer's job was to trim, clean, and remove all mold lines and imperfections in the moist, leathery figure. With a sponge and carving tool, the lines were painstakingly removed with the worker being careful not to make the cuts either too deep or too shallow. These mold lines had to be trimmed just right, for after glazing and the final firing, the lines would show up if not cleaned properly. This essential but time consuming task occupied a department of 10 who employed incentive games to increase productivity. Many of the larger figures were complex and required a great amount of skill and patience. Once the figure was cleaned and all lines removed, the cleaner initialed the bottom of the figure.

Staff member cleans mold lines on bird bath.

Issy Hiner, an artist in her own right, was the head of this department and was responsible for adding freehand trims, such as flowers, ribbons, and hats deemed too delicate to be a component of the whole mold, to ears and tails. These additions were either hand-formed clay or bits of clay that were pressed into a separate, small mold and then painstakingly applied to the figure with clay slip, metal tools, and brushes. The Chinese Court Ladies' hands and jewelry and the large elephants' tails and ears were applied in this manner. One of the staff members admired the large Violet the Elephant but the $45.00 retail price was too high for her. With Braden's permission, Issy converted Violet into the smaller and less expensive Peanuts the Elephant with exact, miniature details. (See pp. 196.)

Saint Francis gets detailed.

The figures had to be moist for cleaning and working purposes. Since figures fresh out of their molds would back up on the production line, they were placed in the damp room to prevent drying. In this canvas-covered chamber a fine mist of water that kept the figures moist and malleable was sprayed. However, if the figures were left too long in the damp room, they would lose their mold detail and crumble apart when handled. The next step for the figures included air or heat drying in infrared dryers to make them firm, forming greenware. Then they would be ready for their first firing trip through the kiln.

The electric tunnel kiln that operated on a slow-moving conveyor belt system was the first of its kind. Long and narrow, the unit was designed by Kay's brother-in-law Alfred Schultz who also helped with the development of the slip colors. Schultz was further responsible for the overhead tubes that dispensed liquid clay through hoses into the molds, eliminating the need for lifting heavy tubs. Heated to 1800 degrees, the kiln was kept running 24 hours a day, loaded twice a day, once in the morning and once in the evening. All of the ceramics were placed in and arranged by height and size. Cones were used to make a second level for smaller figures. The first firing took approximately one work day or eight hours to complete. During this first firing, all water and carbon dioxide were evaporated and the items emerged in hard, stonelike forms called bisque. The bisque ware would be allowed to cool for several hours at the end of firing before being passed to the next department.

The decorating or painting department had a relaxed and casual atmosphere. The figures themselves were painted in lots of 6, 12, or 24, and were brought to the painters on wooden planks. Each decorator had a finished sample decorated by Kay from which to copy the design and coloring. The paint used was actually slip, a liquid form of clay thinned with water and pigmented with color. The slip was thick and gave a raised feel to the figure's surface. The only real paints used were a green and a black, the black being used mostly for the eyes and outline details. The slip colors and hues were developed by Kay and Alfred Schultz. No other ceramic company could duplicate the studio's finishes.

Decorators take break for picture, 1942.

All paint work was performed freehand. No stencils or decals were used so that each piece is, in fact, one-of-a-kind. Painting for Kay Finch was different from painting china because the thick slip would be dropped off the brush and then allowed to flow and form by pushing it with the brush. The flower designs on the pigs Smiley and Grumpy were penciled out by the decorator then filled in with the colored slip in broad strokes, much like tole painting with each one taking about 30 minutes to complete. Variations in color and decoration to the ceramics were added over the years (see photos, p. 82). Many of the pieces have scraffito detail work.

After painting, the decorator would take a sharp pointed instrument and scrape into the colored slip, exposing the underlying clay. This detailing was done for animal fur and on curlicues in decorative costumes and was scraffito work at its best.

Black paint was also finely applied over colored slip for the reverse, thin, dark details. Betty Winckler and Mary Lou Dierker were Kay's top decorators and also heads and trainers of the decorating department. Winckler and Dierker had a penchant for detail and personally decorated many of the intricate figures that required work with tiny brushes and a steady hand. At the end of each day they would check the work of the twelve or more decorators. Any piece that did not satisfy the studio's commitment to quality had to be redone the next day. These painting mistakes could be easily removed by scratching off the slip with a dull knife, leaving the piece ready for repainting. Some of the more advanced decorators were allowed to improvise on some of the designs including the Chinese Court Ladies' flower designs, and Godey dress panels but these had to be approved by Betty before they could be sold. A beginning decorator would work on the small, less complex figures, like the little angels, and had to advance to the detailed Godey couples and others. Maureen Rischard began as a decorator in 1943 and worked on the tiny two-inch pigs. When she reached the detailed Godey figures, she knew she was at the top of the line. "The Godeys

Use of a live model helps bring the subject to life.

were my favorites to decorate. We had Godey pictures and prints from fashion magazines to get ideas on how to decorate these fashionable figures," she recalls.

Each decorator had quotas on how many figures were to be painted each day but the staff were never rushed and were not paid by piece work but were always paid by the hour. Other ceramic operations paid by the piece and the work produced grew fast and sloppy. In order to insure that they would produce a quality product, Kay never attempted to rush her staff. In 1942 a decorator received 50 cents an hour while a skilled mold maker made $3.20.

After decorating, the figures were ready to be dipped in a clear, protective glaze. This mixture of silica was continuously mixed so that its ingredients would not settle. Each figure would be hand dipped into the raw glaze leaving its underside unglazed or bisque. Bowls, vases, and functional items that were completely glazed were placed on small cones as they went through the kiln. Sometimes glaze would be poured into the cavity of the figure for added strength. A second kilning in the conveyor kiln gave the figures a glass-like, protective sheen. The figures were then placed on square trays for their second firing.

Most of the ceramics were marked in some way. Black and red ink stamped marks exist as well as embossed and hand written examples. Paper labels were also used for a time in the early and late 1940s but were most likely peeled off like price tags. After the ceramics had cooled, they were sent to the storage room where they were placed on shelves and put into inventory. The studio had a packing and shipping department, where all orders were received, packed in shredded paper and shipped by weight to retail outlets around the world. A good selection of the ceramics made it to the front sales shop where the public could stop and see the best in California ceramics.

Pat Chapman Hadden was a decorator, painting the many pigs from 1942 to 1944, and also ran the sales shop. The shop had a high ceiling and picture windows that let in the seaside sunlight. Pat always kept the vases filled with fresh flowers from the surrounding garden and Kay's creations lined the shelves and walls. The decorators were located behind a partition that separated them from the shop. "The girls in the decorating department would sit chatting as we painted, then when someone entered the sales shop, everyone became very quiet while I went out to help them," Pat recounts.

Modern sales shop, 1953.

Actresses such as Lucille Ball and Veronica Lake of the famous peek-a-boo hair style would stop by now and then, purchasing several items at a time. Miss Ball fell in love with Petey the Donkey and bought two of them for her yard. They can be seen in some of her family photographs from the late 1940s and early 1950s.

World War II's uncertainty had an effect on everyone, including those who worked for the Finches. "Everyone had someone out in the Pacific, a husband, boyfriend or a brother and you never knew if they were coming back," recalled Lutie Belle Lindeman. V Mail usually got through but some of the girls didn't hear from their men for long periods of time. Blackouts were also a regular occurrence. Shades had to be drawn and one could not drive with your headlights on for fear of night aerial attacks.

For defense reasons the Kay Finch Studio building itself had to be altered. Its design incorporated a sharp point in the roofline above the sales shop. From the air, the U.S. Air Force noticed that this bright white ceramic roof point by coincidence led directly to an important water reservoir and an Air Force base further inland. The building was one of the first along the coast to be camouflaged as precautionary steps were made against enemy action. It was known that enemy spies had listed landmarks of this type so the government had the Finches square off the architectural point.

New camouflaged front of studio, 1942.

The war years were not all scary years as many fun and interesting things happened. Several of the decorators enjoyed becoming pen pals with servicemen, writing letters and receiving responses. One pilot who was stationed at Midway told of the unusual Gooney birds that were all over the island and particularly posed a problem on the aircraft runway. On their own time the girls decided to make their own Gooney sculpture out of miscellaneous items and mailed it off to their pilot pal. From then on the girls nicknamed themselves "The Goons", later producing an in-house newspaper inspired by this theme.

Goons Gaietys Gazette

Printed for the Civies Who Make Pretties for the War Trade

Vol. 1.   Corona del Mar, Calif., Joon 30, 1944   No. 1

THE FINCH FRONT

There's bin sech a lot of talk in these here parts as to whether our ceramics Kirks is meetin the requirements set by our givermint twards the war winnin that we feel we caint let sech subversive talk be circulatin any longer. So we is here presentin a real formal like reeport of the factrys output. PRODUCTION: Goin like mad.

with shipments of ducks.

Navy's shot 10 shipments of hippos into 20 Jap warships and the durn things sunk.

Army Air Corpse dropped 60 shipments of Kay Finch elephants on Berlin and brother they're stampin heck out of theplace.

Fighter pilots has casually slung cherub placks at the dishonorable

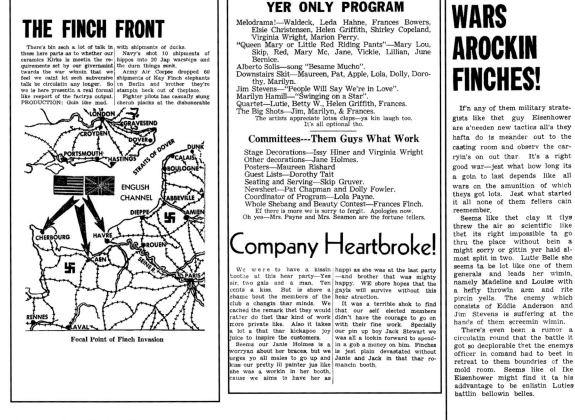

Focal Point of Finch Invasion

YER ONLY PROGRAM

Melodrama!—Waldeck, Leda Hahne, Frances Bowers, Elsie Christensen, Helen Griffith, Shirley Copeland, Virginia Wright, Marion Perry.
"Queen Mary or Little Red Riding Pants"—Mary Lou, Skip, Red, Mary Mc, Jane, Vickie, Lillian, June Bernice.
Alberto Solis—song "Besame Mucho".
Downstairs Skit—Maureen, Pat, Apple, Lola, Dolly, Dorothy, Marilyn.
Jim Stevens—"People Will Say We're in Love".
Marilyn Hamill—"Swinging on a Star".
Quartet—Lutie, Betty W., Helen Griffith, Frances.
The Big Shots—Jim, Marilyn, & Frances.
    The artists appreciate lotsa claps—ya kin laugh too.
    It's all optional tho.

Committees---Them Guys What Work

Stage Decorations—Issy Hiner and Virginia Wright
Other decorations—Jane Holmes.
Posters—Maureen Rishard
Guest Lists—Dorothy Tait
Seating and Serving—Skip Gruver.
Newsheet—Pat Chapman and Dolly Fowler.
Coordinator of Program—Lola Payne.
Whole Shebang and Beauty Contest—Frances Finch.
    Ef there is more we is sorry to fergit. Apologies now.
Oh yea—Mrs. Payne and Mrs. Seamon are the fortune tellers.

Company Heartbroke!

We were to have a kissin boothe at this hear party—Yes sir, two gals and a man. Ten cents a kiss. But is shore a shame bout the members of the club a changin thar minds. We cached the remark thet they would rather do thet thar kind of work more private like. Also it takes a lot a that thar kickapoo joy juice to inspire the customers.

Seems our Janie Holmes is a worryan about her braces, but we urges yo all males to go up and kiss our pretty lil painter jus like she was a workin in her booth, cause we aims to have her as

happi as she was at the last party —and brother that was mighty happy. WE shore hopes that the gayls will survive without this hear atraction.

It was a terrible shok to find that our self elected members didn't have the courage to go on with their fine work. Specially our pin up boy Jack Stewart we was all a lookin forward to spendin a gob a money on him. Finches is jest plain devastated without Janie and Jack in that thar romancin booth.

WARS AROCKIN FINCHES!

If'n any of them military strategists like thet guy Eisenhower are a'needen new tactics all's they hafta do is meander out to the casting room and observ the carryin's on out thar. It's a right good war—jest what how long its a goin to last depends like all wars on the amunition of which theys got lots. Jest what started it all none of them fellers cain reemember.

Seems like thet clay it flys threw the air so scientific like thet its right impossible ta go thru the place without bein a might sorry or gittin yer haid almost split in two. Lutie Belle she seems ta be lot like one of them generals and leads her wimin, namely Madeline and Louise with a hefty throwin arm and rite pircin yells. The enemy which consists of Eddie Anderson and Jim Stevens is suffering at the hands of them screemin wimin.

There's even been a rumor a circulatin round that the battle it got so deeplorable thet the enemys officer in comand had to beet in retreat to them boundries of the mold room. Seems like ol Ike Eisenhower might find it ta his addvantage to be enlistin Luties battlin bellowin belles.

Excerpts from Vol. 1, No. 1.

An Air Corps pilot friend of one decorator would buzz the studio in order to attract the girl's attention, flying low over the roof. Braden had to tell the decorator to have her friend stop terrorizing the place. He also had to deal with production abandonment each time military troop convoys would pass by the studio on their way to Camp Pendleton. All the girls, and that was well more than half the staff, would run out to the porch and every open window to wave and cheer for the men defending their country.

Break and rest periods allowed the staff a chance to relax on the wide open patios that overlooked the ocean. Cold drinks and fresh fruit from the Finches' trees were served and sometimes a group would pack their lunch and run down to the beach to eat. Braden was extremely flexible with the staff and their schedules. Several times he allowed workers to come in early, one time at 4 a.m., so that they could leave early for a trip to Palm Springs. Kay and Braden felt that the "worker is always right" in the production of their product and this held true in keeping happy everyone who was employed there. The studio was designed with the comfort of the worker in mind because Braden felt that, "To produce a beautiful product one must be able to work in an atmosphere of beauty and harmony of design." Further, Braden believed superior quality work would result from better working conditions. The studio was always clean, with wide windows and colorful furniture that made everyone feel welcomed and appreciated. Also the Finches and "The Goons" held events and dances at the studio and other locations.

Staff on patio with bisque figures.

The Finches themselves enjoyed parties and hosted many quite regularly, with one and all invited. Decorator Jane Holmes Ross remembers the goat barbeque, a Mexican style feast where a whole goat was cooked in a pit on the cliffs behind the studio. "Dances were popular on the studio's large patios with Kay, Braden, and everyone joining in and the Christmas parties were wonderful," she recalls. Each Christmas Kay would put up a large tree reaching high to the ceiling in the sales shop. "She would create special ceramic ornaments, different for each year. During the war real trees and tinsel were hard to come by so one year Kay decorated a cedar tree with coral pink ceramic seafoam star ornaments and lights that became the showstopper of the harbor area," Jane remembers.

At some of the larger parties stage acts would be presented on the lawn with Kay and staff singing. Whole production numbers would be staged with beauty contests, funny skits, and more. The Finches were so solicitous of their staff's happiness at work that they even built mold maker Skee his own work studio behind the building.

Kay and Braden dressed for costume party.

The evenings and weekends were filled with fun and frolics, for while 1940s Orange County enjoyed a more relaxed life style, slower paced than it is today, there was also an active nightlife. These young women and men roller-skated and biked along the coast during the day but at night, a more glittery Orange County emerged. The Rendezvous Room on Balboa Peninsula was the hot spot for listening and dancing to all the big bands, including Stan Kenton and Glen Miller. In fact during the early 1940s, the Newport Beach-Balboa Bay-Corona del Mar tri-cities were the Riviera of the western United States or Beverly-Hills-by-the-Sea.

Before Las Vegas, this area was a swinging spot where stars such as Judy Garland and Mickey Rooney entertained at the beachfront Cabrillo Dance Pavilion and gambling was a part of the night life scene. Orange County was a local get-away spot for tired Angelenos as well as Army, Navy, Marine, and Air Force-based servicemen and women. Service units such as the Santa Ana Army Air Corps Replacement Center, the Navy Lighter-than-Air Station, El Toro Marine Corps Air Station, Los Alamitos Naval Air Station, the Naval Ammunition and Net Depot at Seal Beach, the Coast Guard Station at San Clemente, and the United States Marine Corps unit at Camp Pendleton populated the area.

One of the most popular clubs was Christian's Hut which boasted restaurants in both Balboa and Corona del Mar. Other well-known places for dining and dancing were the Blue Room, the Balboa Inn, the Castaways (long before Gilligan), the Bamboo Room, Vaux Restaurant, and the fabled Dilhman's.

In the mid 1950s for a special occasion, Finch patrons and staff could have the opportunity of dining at the Vaux Restaurant at 1918 prices. One penny bought soup or salad or coffee and a Delmonico steak went for seventy-five cents, the whole dinner for a grand total of seventy-eight taxless cents. Those good old days could be really good!

Corona del Mar itself had its own special history with tales of pirate landings on the beach when the area had been named Rocky Point. It was a colorful area even back in the days when it was a part of old Rancho San Joaquin during the time of Spanish rule. By the 1940s, Corona del Mar, the Crown of the Sea, formerly called Palisades City, featured not only a lovely coastline but a noteworthy restaurant of its own. This establishment, owned by Fred and Margaret Atkinson, was called the Hurley Bell, and named for an old English tavern located at Hurley-on-Thames. It was situated right next door to the Finch Studio. Margaret Atkinson was well-known not only for her restaurant's cuisine, bar and gambling, but also for the giant parrot always perched atop her shoulder. Husband Fred never put in an appearance and was always said to be out fishing. The restaurant was sold to Lawry's in 1945 and later became the present-day five star establishment Five Crowns.

Located between Balboa and Laguna, the Finch Studio attracted locals, tourists, and celebrities alike on their way from the Balboa Fun Zone down to the famed Laguna Festival of the Arts, a play at the Laguna Playhouse or a leisurely dinner at the old Victor Hugo. It was a period of dynamic activity in a place filled with great energy and all of this excitement was communicated to the little studio by the sea and filtered through its work force into the work they produced.

Every summer the tourists, or "brown baggers" as the locals called them, would come to Balboa and Corona del Mar. The population of these beach communities would then swell from the winter average of a couple hundred to several thousand. Newport Bay was popular with everyone for its boating, fishing, and especially swimming. In fact, to save the five cent fare it cost to take the ferry across the bay to Lido Island, many kids would just jump in and swim their way across.

The coastal communities of Newport Beach, Corona del Mar and in particular Laguna Beach had, through the years, become artists' colonies, producing an abundance of ceramic studios and small factories located in garages and the backs of cottages. This ceramics trade was a true cottage industry. Many of these people produced quality ware while others couldn't reach that mark. Kay, Braden and their staff knew that they had the best in quality and craftsmanship in the area and possibly the whole country.

Big Corona Beach, 1940s.

In the Finch attention to quality, all the ceramics were assigned numbers and over time some even found names. Every so often Kay would dub a creation with a name. The large rooster Chanticleer was also known as Bobby Sox. Other times the staff would have a competition to name a new ceramic. With the contest judged by Kay and Braden, the winner would receive one of the new figures as the prize. In 1945 the Ruth Sloan Shops decided that the names enhanced the character of the ceramics and made them even more buyer-friendly. Soon everybody knew about the pottery pigs Winkie and Sassy, the ducks Peep and Jeep and the most popularly produced ceramic poultry, Biddy and Butch.

With the war's end in September of 1945, servicemen returned. Many of the girls got married and settled down to raising families. At the studio some stayed on and new decorators and other personnel were soon hired to replace the ones who had left. Through it all, the studio continued to produce Kay's popular ceramics, adding new items to the line for the next sixteen years, and adding new enthusiasts with each passing year.

While other ceramic outfits closely guarded their production secrets, Kay and Braden decided to open their operation to the public for studio tours every Tuesday afternoon at 2 o'clock. Interested visitors could view all the processes of pottery manufacturing as a staff member guided them through the studio, explaining each step in the making of a Finch ceramic.

The studio produced unique kidney shaped tables that offered indentations in their surface for flower arrangements and displays. At this point many ceramic studios were trying hard to survive the competition. The Finch operation kept changing and continued to be profitable. They introduced larger decorative items and color-coordinated bowls, vases and figures. Yet as these changes took place, the staff decreased. In 1947 over 65 were employed at the studio while in 1951, 30 employees were on staff.

At this time the rare luster paints were used to decorate the figures. These shimmery colors were thinly applied with broad strokes much like regular painting. The lusters were dull in color when applied to the bisque figure. Once they were glazed the colors became iridescent and shiny. Limited decorating reigned through the late 1950s with most figures and bowls dipped in color glaze.

In the last months of the studio, most of the remaining staff left. Actual production had ended in the fall of 1961 when Braden became ill and the studio's final close-out sale began in December 1962. If the studio had been born like a lion in the hurly-burly years of pre-World War II, it seemed to disappear quietly like one of those gentle lambs Kay had so joyfully created and produced.

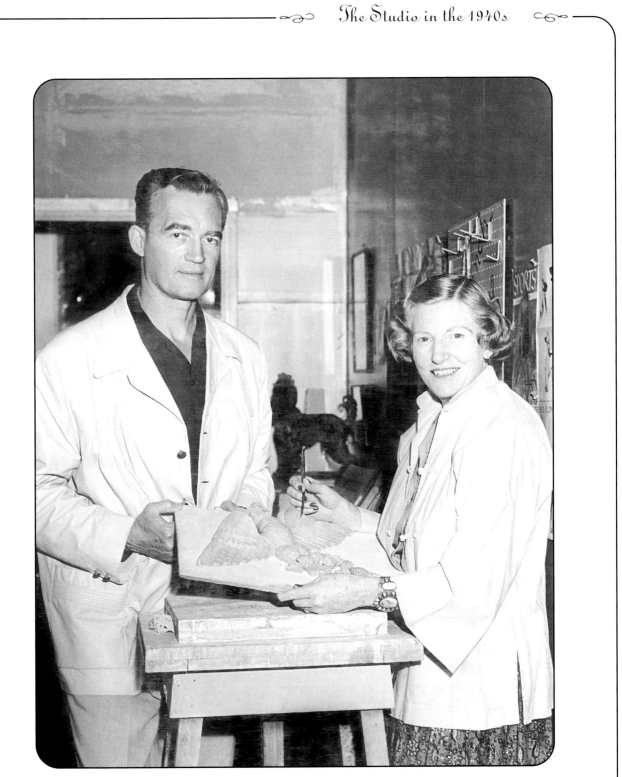

Kay and Braden working on eagle wall plaque, #5904, 1959.

Variations, Collecting and Displaying

Variations in decorating and added details exist extensively throughout the Kay Finch line. Many of the designs were produced for long periods of time and changes were made over the years to increase sales through variety. Changes were made in the studio manufacturing also to prevent boredom from infecting a decorating staff with the duty of painting the same design over and over. The following pages feature information and photos on some of these variations. Those popular pigs, Winkie, Sassy, Smiley, Grumpy and Grandpa among others, were produced as figures and banks from 1940 to 1951 and can be found with several, different floral designs including daisies, carnations, violets, and geraniums. In the mid 1940s, a larger floral peasant design was introduced and became popular. The pigs also have been found with California fruit designs featuring wild strawberries and personalized versions with children's names, and late 1940s and early 1950s solid color examples have also been discovered.

As with the pigs, the most noticeable variations occur with standard items produced for a good length of time. The angels 114 a, b, c were among the first in production in Santa Ana in 1937 and were produced for about 14 years. Although the designs themselves didn't change, the painting styles did.

For a brief time in the 1940s, the studio offered many of the animal figures both in pastels and in natural colors or grays. At this point, the buying public preferred Kay's original pastels to the natural and gray adaptation with fewer orders received for the muted tones.

All the decorators were taught to copy a certain style and the look of the line remained uniform, but some of the decorators were admittedly more skilled than others. Many collectors look for the work of one decorator in particular, Mary Lou Dierker. Although the decorators were never allowed to sign the pieces they painted, Mary Lou's work can be easily recognized. Her tight style and intricate, detailed line work are unsurpassed. Kay's work itself is most eagerly sought and highly prized when found. She did not do any production painting in the studio but did all prototypes, decorator samples, color variations, and special gifts to family and friends in her private studio. She also did all of the early production work in Santa Ana in 1937 and 1938. Many of these pieces bear her initials, her full name, a special message from Braden and her and/or the word "sample." Kay's decorating tends to be lighter, softer, and more intricate than the production pieces. She also liked to use fine gold detailing over glaze on most of her work. Kay would sometimes take a plain greenware figure and customize it by adding special details and decorating style (see photo, p. 130). Though limited in number, ceramics decorated by Kay do find their way into the market place. Note that ceramics with Kay's penned signature don't necessarily mean that they were decorated by her since she would sometimes sign studio production pieces for friends, but these also are rare.

Mary Lou Dierker, one of Kay's top decorators, 1949.

Ceramic piggies.

Variations are not limited simply to decorations. Different clay hues were also used including the soft pink and white. In the late 1940s a yellow pottery base was introduced in the baby line. The American Indian family is unique since the clay used in these 1944 pieces is a natural terra cotta that Native Americans might use in their own pottery. Later examples were made in the standard tinted clay. Terra cotta clay was also used on the earlier Mexican peasant tots of 1940.

Lamb and quail in sand matte glaze.

Indian mother and child in pink-tinted clay.

By 1948 the line included over 200 designs with well over half of them being "active" or popular sellers. Most designs were kept in the line to offer variety for the buyers even if they were not big sellers. These slow sellers were produced in lesser quantities or only if they were ordered. But some, even the popular ones just didn't make it for a number of reasons and sometimes were removed soon after their introduction. The breakfast sets featuring the flower patterns Blue Daisy and Briar Ross and the California Calico and Corral dinner patterns, inspired by the rustic countryside of mountainous Julian, were added in 1946 and 1947 but were quickly removed from the line about 1949. Their high cost and large size filled the kiln's valuable spaces. The long-tailed pheasant was replaced with a short-tailed one about 1950 because of constant replacement due to tail breakage in shipping. Other special items found not to be extensively produced include an angel candleholder, Mexican and Russian boys and girls, a donkey with bells, a U.S. sailor figure, a child with a drum and the ceramic mantel clocks.

Briar Rose breakfast set introduced in 1946.

Kay did many one-of-a-kind items that have stayed in the collections of family, friends, and associates. These pieces include original intricate sculptures in clay and bronze, paintings, sketches, Christmas cards, and specially decorated production pieces. One very unique piece is the Band Wagon. Executed by Kay in 1942, this original sculpture was a 20th anniversary gift to Braden and features a horse drawn wagon with costumed drivers, band members, and circus animals. Close inspection of the fine detail will reveal initials and names of friends and staff members on each figure. Kay and Braden are, of course, the drivers.

The Band Wagon sculpture.

Christmas card, 1974.

Kay's hand-produced Christmas card, 1950.

By the 1950s, individuals and retail outlets could special-order certain items with a choice of coloring, personalizing, and gold detailing. The cocker spaniel Vicki has been found personalized with a dog tag that reads "Tootsie." As with most of the other canine figures, Vicki came in a wide range of colors and finishes.

The store buyers bought only what sold, so Kay Finch made in mass what they bought. Some items were produced for over ten years because of their popularity with the public while others were made for only a short period of time. In the collector's market today, rarity and availability of any item can be due to several factors including loss and damage, availability in established collections, and higher or lower initial studio sales in any given area. With the 1950s introduction of the home decorator solid color, high glazes, lusters and pink pearl, many of the original 1940s ceramic pieces were discontinued. Because of rising costs, an abundance of the clay detail work was also dropped. With the new bowls, vases, planters, dog figures, and holiday items which were now the mainstay of the line, large amounts were done in solid colors which were simpler to produce.

On the subject of scarcity, it is believed that items introduced in the late 1940s are harder to find because they were produced for less time than ceramics introduced in the early part of that decade. The same may hold true for ceramics made a year or two before the close of the studio in 1962, though this is not substantiated. The catalog model numbers generally tell when a ceramic was introduced. Three digit numbers were created before 1946, four digit numbers from 1946 on with the first two numerals indicating the year it was introduced or assigned a number. For example, #4715 would most likely have been brought out in 1947.

Chinese boy and girl displayed with bowl.

Christmas ceramics in lusters and golds, 1952.

Research has found that these model numbers are not always accurate about the year when an item was introduced. The Madonna and Babe are given the numbers 4900 and 4900A, stating that they were added to the line in 1949, when in actuality they were produced from 1940 to about 1952. One reason might be that these figures weren't added to the sales catalog until 1949. These catalog model numbers never appear on the actual production pieces themselves.

Copies and imitations are abundant in the second market but fortunately they can easily be differentiated from the true article. Kay's creations were very popular so it was understandable and somewhat flattering that look-alikes and direct rip-offs would arrive on the scene. The practice began locally with several mom and pop ceramic operations trying to be successful. Then larger domestic and foreign companies, especially those from Japan, jumped on the band wagon, but none of the plagiarized work could come close to Kay's original accomplishments. These reproductions were made in several ways. When the used molds were discarded, scavengers would dig them out for reuse. After this practice was discovered, Braden made the staff destroy the used molds. Another way to copy was to make a new mold from a Finch ceramic figure. These pieces tend to be smaller in size and have less figure detail due to shrinkage.

About 1960 the Finches gave in to the continued onslaught of fakes and began offering unfired greenware figures and glazes to hobbyists and interested parties. These ceramics could be taken home or to school, decorated the way the artist chose and fired in his own kiln. Large amounts of these ceramics can be found, namely the rooster and chickens, but the decorating and glazing are not of the same consistency and quality of Kay's creations and the hobbyists' works are easy to differentiate from the real studio pieces.

Please note that Freeman McFarlin later purchased several of Kay's original molds, including the owls, chickens, Asian people, dogs, and others, for production in their standard finishes. These are classified Kay Finch Freeman McFarlin (see next chapter).

Not all of the Kay Finch ceramics are marked since some are too small or paper labels have been lost. After searching and much careful observation, you will become an expert on Kay's work and better able to appreciate the value of the real pieces.

The how, what, and why of collecting Kay Finch is a complete story in itself. Many people may collect the figures because they grew up with them or simply because they are drawn by the pieces' charm and humor. Some collectors only seek dogs while others search out feline figures. For some Finch fanciers, whatever the category, nothing will do but the animal figurines. This group never collects the human figures. Then there are the more broad-minded people who collect all the figures, both human and animal. The true "Finchophile" is the collector who appreciates everything the studio ever produced and will collect all that is available. Availability is the key word because most of Kay's ceramics are not easy to find.

Probably there are several different reasons for the relative scarcity of Kay Finch art. The studio was always a small operation by the standards of the day's most prominent ceramic companies. The staff turned out about 150 pieces per day at the peak of its popularity, with the studio shipping its product to every state in the union as well as twenty-one foreign countries. Kay Finch was exceptionally popular in both South America and Central America. Consequently, these pieces are a lost cause for American collectors.

In addition, many households with a cache of Finch art tend to "keep it in the family."

Often these treasured pieces are handed down in the family as heirlooms. The dedicated collector can meet a great deal of resistance in the market place where people are delighted to describe or even exhibit their pieces but are definitely less willing to part with them.

A further factor in the scarcity of the ceramics is the unfortunate reality of loss through attrition. Californians lose many ceramics to such natural disasters as earthquakes, fires, and floods. Because of the subject matter of some of the figures, the art was given as gifts to children and breakage with children is a fact of life. Planters, fountains, and some of the larger ceramic figures were placed outdoors with resultant trauma to many of the pieces.

St. Francis with bird bath.

In the early days of ceramics, broken figures were just thrown away and thus lost to the owner and future collectors. Due to the wonderful quality of the restoration work we have today, damaged pieces can be sent back to the shelf instead of the trash bin.

For the true "Finchophile" then, the real thrill lies in finding a new piece and working out settings for displaying the art. Kay herself often demonstrated decorating tips in her production line. She coordinated the colors of trays and bowls with the figures in order to insure beautiful and distinctive table settings and she also strongly believed in mixing and matching her own art with that of others as well. Often one ceramic piece or a small group will work well. A solo piece can make quite a statement.

One of the pleasures of assembling a Finch collection is the process of matching the figures with the different bowls and architectural pieces. It's fun to let one's own imagination and creativity blend with Kay's ceramics. Whether one lines the figures on a shelf or settles them in a china cabinet or populates the entire house with different displays, the pleasure Kay Finch gives is still very much with us.

Pen and ink Afghan, 1972.

Freeman McFarlin

Many people mistakenly assume that the art of Kay Finch ended with the closing of her studio in 1963. In fact, the pottery production part of Kay's life took other avenues.

Kay continued to produce her art on an informal basis. For her friends and for her own enjoyment, the artist created embroidery work, bronze sculptures, canine motif jewelry, and beautiful needlepoint designs, fashioning wonderful portraits of some of the famous dogs of Crown Crest Kennels along with other subjects. She also painted portraits.

In 1963, Kay sold some of her design molds to Freeman McFarlin, a local pottery concern, believing at that time that she was closing the door on any further production design of her own. Work with Crown Crest Kennels and many other interests fully occupied her days and Kay continued to find the hands-on work with the dogs as satisfying in its way as the designing of her animal models had always been.

Freeman McFarlin had maintained a successful ceramic operation in the city of El Monte, California, from 1927 when it was founded by Gerald McFarlin. In 1951, Maynard Anthony Freeman joined the company as a designer and the two men very successfully united their resources and talents.

The Freeman McFarlin company had experienced some acclaim with a line of distinctive animals created by Freeman himself. Hoping to expand their product base and ensure added success, the company sought to buy the Kay Finch molds, at once recognizing not only the value of the Finch line itself, but also the intrinsic cachet of the Finch name. Therefore, in 1963, Freeman McFarlin purchased the Finch molds, actually turning out about fifty production pieces with a numbering sequence from 801 through 849.

It's quite easy to distinguish an original Kay Finch figure from that of one produced by Freeman McFarlin from the very same mold. Kay used her own inimitable glazes, tints, and design touches such as the trademark curlicues and expressive eye detailing. In its production process, Freeman McFarlin used thick white and cream glazes, gold leaf with hints of ochre peeping through, dark olive greens or even dramatic kelly greens. Little touches such as painted bills on gold-leaf birds and lacquered eyes often highlighted the Freeman McFarlin efforts. While these Finch reissues proved popular, many customers still wished for original designs created by Kay Finch herself. So in the mid 1960s, Kay's aficionados had something to cheer about when the artist agreed to design some new pieces for the company. By this time, Freeman McFarlin had closed the old El Monte factory and was operating solely out of the modern San Marcos facility they had opened in 1968.

The pieces which Kay Finch designed for the company are radically different from her own earlier work. They are definitely more realistic. On some figures, the dogs display complete anatomical detail. In general, the models are larger and sturdier in appearance than Kay's own studio efforts. The glazes are distinctively different as well, ranging from those previously discussed to one of a clear, almost porcelain-like white finish.

Kay with Afghan friend, summer, 1983.

Kay, still creating, late 1970s.

While designing for Freeman McFarlin, Kay created figures of dogs, kangaroos, rabbits, and other animals. The artist also designed decorative tiles, producing pieces for the company for a period of about fifteen years, from 1965 to 1980. She then retired for good. This period of creative reincarnation proved to be a memorable time. It was destined to be Kay's last burst of creative endeavor for the general public.

The works which she produced clearly demonstrate that the artistic and creative spark remained strong and intact in Kay. The absolute joy she gained in sharing her love of animals is apparent in each figure.

Obviously, the Kay Finch figures created for Freeman McFarlin are regarded differently from her earlier work. Indeed, some collectors may not even be aware of their existence. The difference goes far beyond the change in glazes or decorative touches. It's a much more serious artist who is displayed in these works, one with far less whimsy in evidence.

In the Freeman McFarlin art, one sees the accurate, realistic workmanship of a mature artist still in full possession of a unique artistic ability and viewpoint. These works are representational with fewer humorous touches to beguile the viewer. Nothing distracts from the basic strength of the art itself. In the future, these creations will most probably be as eagerly sought by collectors as the better-known pieces from the studio years. As collectors learn of their existence, the search will be on for these ceramic "sleepers." The Freeman McFarlin-Kay Finch connection is also well worth searching out because of its ultimate historical interest. It comprises the final chapter in the unique art of Kay Finch.

Whippet and Rudiki done in Freeman McFarlin finishes, 1975.

Kay's dining room, early 1980s.

11¾", Vicki, cocker spaniel in black and white, #455. *$600.00 – 700.00*

18", Best in show Afghan, #5490. *$2,000.00 – 3,000.00*

Afghan head, #476. *$1,000.00 – 1,500.00*

8", Poodle beggar, #5262. *$300.00 – 350.00*

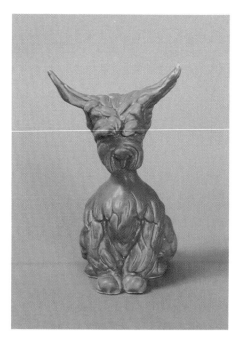

6½", Silly skye terrier in orange matte glaze, #5926. *$150.00 – 200.00*

16", Perky poodle, #5419. *$1,200.00 – 1,800.00*

Sitting Afghan, #5553. *$250.00 – 350.00*

10", Afghan head without base in shades of white, brown, and gray. *$1,000.00 – 1,500.00*

Yorky pups, #170 and 171. *$450.00 – 550.00 pair*

5", Wind-blown Afghan in green, #5757. *$200.00 – 300.00*

13", Show dog a.k.a. Rudiki, #5082. This figure was done by Kay herself and is a tribute to her prize-winning Afghan. *$800.00 – 1,000.00*

Dog Show A.K.C. Champions: Afghan, #5016, Cocker, #5003, and Boxer, #5025. *$200.00 – 250.00 each*

Cigarette jar with attached yorky, #4766, yorky figure, #4851. *$200.00 – 250.00 each*

8", Pup, #5320. *$300.00 – 400.00*

8", Two versions of cocker, #5201. *$300.00 – 350.00 each*

11", Cocker, #455. This one is personalized "Tootsie" with gold details and her own dog dish. *$600.00 – 700.00*

14" long, Pekingese, #154. *$450.00 – 550.00*

Airedales, in red and black combination, and in platinum finish that could be special ordered. Part of A.K.C. dog show, #4832. *$200.00 – 350.00*

10", Playful poodles, in tanbark and pink lusters, #5203 and #5204. *$700.00 – 800.00 pair*

"Little Angel" Afghans, #4911 and #4964. *$200.00 – 350.00 each*

5", Yorky, #170, and Doggie, #5301, in lusters. *$225.00 – 375.00 each*

13", Show Dog (Rudiki), #5082. *$800.00 – 1,000.00*

10", Pomeranian Mitzi, #465. *$600.00 – 700.00*

7", Foo dog, #5601. *$400.00 – 500.00*

17½", Coach Dog in all his spotted glory, #159. *$1,500.00 – 2,000.00*

2" center, three Afghan head pins, #5081. *$200.00 – 250.00 each.*

11", Yorkshire Terrier, (Puddin'), #158. *$1,200.00 – 1,500.00*

Afghan, #4830. *$250.00 – 350.00*

One-of-a-kind Afghan. *NPA*

Two versions of Yorky Pup, one with platinum finish, #171. *$225.00 – 375.00 each*

23" l. x 13" h., Whippet, #5920. *$800.00 – 1,000.00*

4" to 6", three Percherons, #130 a, b, and c. *$100.00 – 150.00 each*

11", Colt, #4806. *$250.00 – 350.00*

Stallion with no base, #213. *$1,500.00 – 3,500.00*

20", Stallion tang horse in all his trappings, #213. *$1,500.00 – 3,500.00*

30", Petey the Donkey, #4776. *$2,000.00 – 3,000.00*

Western burros, #4768, and #4769. *$100.00 – 150.00 each*

6", Jezebel, in pastels and natural grays, #179. $200.00 – 250.00

Donkey, with decorated, detailed mane, #135. $100.00 – 200.00

Burro, #475. Can a burro ever be graceful? This one is. $250.00 – 350.00

8½", Mehitabel the playful cat, #181. $350.00 – 400.00

10", Anna the Siamese Cat, #5103.
$350.00 – 400.00

10", Ambrosia Cat, #155. $450.00 –
500.00

Baby Ambrosia, #5164, Jezzy, #5302,
and small cat. $150.00 – 200.00 each

Jezzy in slip colors, #5302.
$150.00 – 200.00

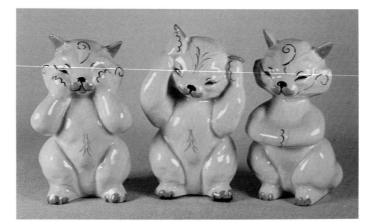

3", Do no evil, hear no evil, and see no evil cats, #4834, #4835, and #4836. *$300.00 – 400.00 set of three*

11¾", Cookie Puss with collar, #4614. *$1,200.00 – 2,000.00*

3½", Tiny Cat, #157, and 2½", Peke, #156. *$100.00 – 125.00 each*

Mr. Tom, 1962, a large watch-cat. *$1,200.00 – 1,800.00*

3¼", Puff and Muff, #183 and #182. *$75.00 – 90.00 each*

Baby Ambrosia, very detailed, #5164. *$150.00 – 200.00*

10¼", Hannibal, the angry cat, #180. *$450.00 – 600.00*

17", Violet, queen of the circus, #190. *$2,000.00 – 2,500.00*

4", Small elephant, #5304. *$150.00 – 200.00*

Elephant trio, 4½", #4805,
5", #4626, and 4½", #4804.
$150.00 – 200.00 each

Elephants: 8½", Peanuts,
#191. 6¾", Pop Corn, #192.
Both in circus design.
$450.00 – 650.00 pair

3", Two versions of small circus elephants,
#5364. *$150.00 – 200.00 each*

Trunk talk with Peanuts #191 and Pop Corn #192 with flower-filled ears. *$450.00 – 650.00 pair*

11", Rabbit "Cuddles", #4623. *$350.00 – 450.00*

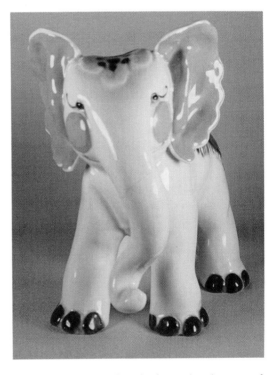

6¾", Pop Corn, the elephant, in circus garb with fringe instead of tassels. *NPA*

Variant of Listening Bunny in pink and white, minus bow, #452. *$250.00 – 350.00*

8½", Listening Bunny, #452 and 8½", Carrots, #473, all ready for the lettuce patch. *$500.00 – 700.00*

Cottontail, painted by Kay herself in antiqued-gold finish and signed, an artistic doodle. #152. *NPA*

2½", Three variations, Cottontail Baby, #152. *$75.00 – 125.00 each*

Skunks, #4774 and #4775. *$350.00 – 550.00 pair*

Skunks, #4774 and #4775 in variant brown and white. *$350.00 – 550.00 pair*

10", Maybe two monkey's uncles, #4962 and #4903. *$450.00 – 600.00 each*

3½", Socko, #4842, and Jocko, #4841, ready for their circus act. Decorated and signed by Kay. *$250.00 – 350.00 pair*

4½", Two versions of Socko, #4841. *$125.00 – 175.00 each*

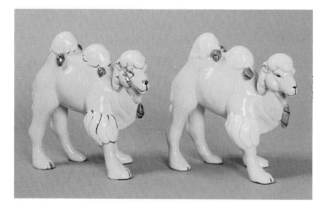

5", Camels, very detailed, "ships of the desert," #464. *$250.00 – 350.00 each*

4", Sleepy bear, #5004. *$200.00 – 250.00*

5", Bear, hard-to-find figure, one of a pair, #4847. *$300.00 – 350.00*

3" to 4", Squirrels, #108a and b. *$150.00 – 200.00 pair*

10", A screwy squirrel, about ten of which were produced. *$1,200.00 – 1,500.00*

Standing lamb, #109 and two kneeling lambs #136, one early version. *$75.00 – 125.00 each*

10½", Prancing lamb with hand-applied flower garland around neck, #168. *$550.00 – 650.00*

2", Turtle, three versions: Top right, papa turtle, #125; bottom center, baby turtle, #126; top left, variation of baby turtle, #126, *$100.00 – 150.00 each*

2", Three versions of guppy fish, #173. *$75.00 – 125.00 each*

1½" h. x 8½" l., Guppy, detailed photo, #173. *$75.00 – 125.00*

Detail of fish and starfish crown on seal's head.

24" overall, Seal or manatee fountain, #6001, and 8" shell fount base, #6002. *$2,000.00 – 2,500.00*

10" h. x 16" l., Grandpa Pig covered in flowers, #163. *$600.00 – 800.00*

Pigs: 3½", Sassy, #166; 3¾", 6", Grumpy, #165; 6¾", Smiley, #164; 3¾", Winkie, #185; trough, #4660. Smaller pigs *$100.00 – 125.00 each.* Trough, *$50.00 – 75.00.* Larger pigs, *$300.00 – 350.00 each.*

Salt and Pepper Pigs, #131, and Bitsy Pigs, #130. *$50.00 – 150.00 each*

Small garlanded piggie, #5055.
$125.00 – 175.00 each

15", Tropicana Cockatoo, decorated by
Kay for a special friend, #5401. *$550.00
– 750.00*

4", Small bird, circa 1950. *NPA*

4", Dicky birds, a and b,
#4905. *$125.00 – 150.00 each*

4½" and 3", Mr. and Mrs. Bird, #453 and #454. *$150.00 – 200.00 pair*

Little pheasants, #5355. *$75.00 – 100.00 each*

3½", Mr. Bird, in pink and mauve, #453, *$75.00 – 100.00*, with color-coordinated flower dish, #4729. *$50.00 – 75.00*

5", Parakeet, #5403. *$200.00 – 250.00*

16", Long-tailed Pheasant, difficult to produce because of its fragile tail, #5020 or #153. *$400.00 – 550.00*

Tanbark and gold short-tailed pheasant, circa 1950, #5300. *$450.00 – 550.00*

3½", Pink swan ashtray, #4958.
4¼" l., pink leaf ashtray, #4730.
$50.00 – 75.00 each

Penguins: 7½", Pete #466; 4¾", Polly, #467; and 3¼", Pee Wee, #468. Makes a fine polar family. *$600.00 – 750.00 set of three*

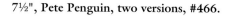

7½", Pete Penguin, two versions, #466.

10¾" h., Chanticleer, #129. Also known as Bobby Socks. *$350.00 – 400.00*

Dove on a napkin ring. *NPA*

Mr. and Mrs. Banty, different color schemes, #4844, and #4843. *$200.00 – 250.00 pair*

Butch and Biddy, #176 and #177. *$250.00 – 300.00 pair*

8" x 5", Doves in tanbark and gold, #5101; two versions of #5102. *$250.00 – 300.00 pair*

Quacky and Wacky, #471 and #472. *$350.00 – 550.00 pair*

4 ½" h., Quacky, #472. A dramatic variant color scheme is shown on this example.

"Ducky", #5006, and egg, #6010. *$100.00 – 150.00 each*

3", Ducks, Peep and Jeep, #178a and b. *$75.00 – 125.00 pair*

Original relief of Afghan done for a piece of furniture. *NPA*

8½", Hoot, #187; 6¾", Toot, #188, and 3¾", Tootsie, #189. *$300.00 – 350.00 set of three*

Hoot, Toot, and Tootsie in variant colors.

3", Tootsie shakers, #189. *$100.00 – 150.00 pair*

Tiny owl. *$75.00 – 100.00*

Ceramic dicky bird clock, no works, circa 1949. *NPA*

Ceramic cuckoo clock, circa 1945. *NPA*

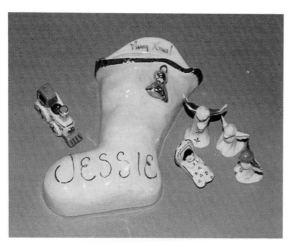

Personalized Christmas Stocking
and tiny angels, hand painted.
$100.00 – 200.00 each

Planter, with seated lamb, Baby's
First from California line, #5116.
$75.00 – 125.00

Jocko, #4841, attached to contain-
er, #5116. *$150.00 – 200.00*

5½", Kneeling choir boy, #211. Back and front detail. *$100.00 – 125.00.* Boy on right decorated and signed by Kay. *NPA*

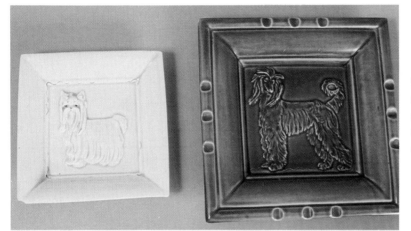

7¾", Yorkshire ashtray/plaque, #5332, and tanbark Afghan ashtray/plaque. *$75.00 – 100.00 each*

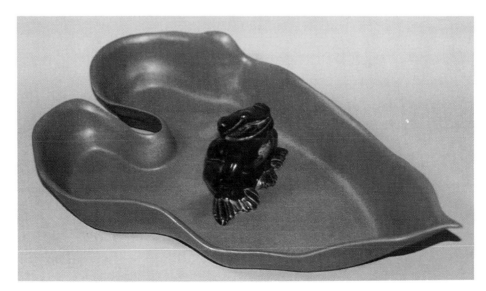

3½", Leaf dish, with teakwood laughing frog, #5009. *$100.00 – 150.00 each*

7", Mink, decorated by Kay Finch. A special piece, #5924. *NPA. Undecorated, $250.00 – 350.00*

Horse head salt and pepper shakers. *$150.00 – 200.00 pair*

Chipmunks, never put into production. Unpainted one was used as a glaze tester. *NPA*

5" Hippos, produced with flowers, bows, and birds, #5019. *$250.00 – 300.00 each*

Hippo, with neck bow, without flowers in his mouth, #5019. *$250.00 – 300.00*

Hippo, without flower in mouth, #5019, and Elephant, in sand matte finish, circa early 1950s, #4626. *$175.00 – 225.00 each*

10", One of the three wise men, #5592. Figure's gift to the holy child is missing. *$175.00 – 225.00*

12" h., Large conch shell, #4619.
$75.00 – 125.00

Covered Easter egg boxes and tiny chicks popping out of eggshells. *$75.00 – 125.00 each*

Early jar or canister, circa 1940.
$75.00 – 150.00

Dog steins featuring Afghan or poodle as handles, #5458. *$150.00 – 200.00 each*

7½", Stein with poodle handle. This piece could also serve as a vase.

Afghan plaque. *$175.00 – 225.00*

Ashtray designed as a trophy for dog show winners. The letters S.A.V.K.C. stand for "Santa Ana Valley Kennel Club" which Kay often mentioned in her dog show magazine column. *$75.00 – 125.00*

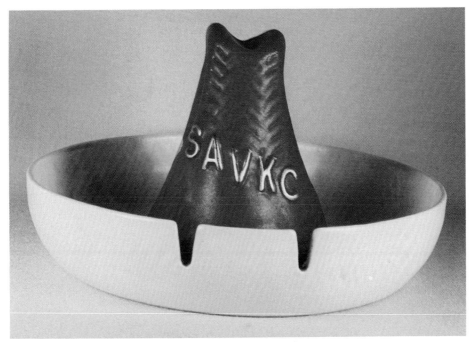

9" diameter, Sombrero, with matte finish. It sports a paper label indicating that it was an award given to a best-in-breed Japanese spaniel. Relief letters stand for "Santa Ana Valley Kennel Club." Probably from the late 1950s-early 1960s. Rare piece. *NPA*

Copper medallion, Afghan Hound Club of California, designed by Kay, given as trophies, highly prized. *NPA*

4¾", Afghan plaque, inscribed "Kay Finch 1949" and cast in silver on copper. Created as a trophy which Kay's own dog probably won, #4955. *NPA*

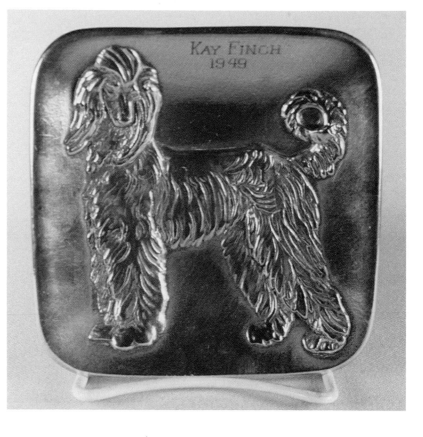

Angel, #140a. *$150.00 – 200.00*

Topsy turvy angel, #140b.
$150.00 – 200.00

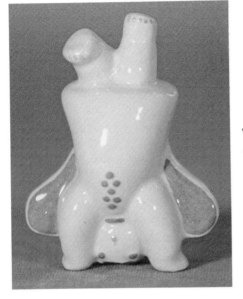

9", Madonna in matte glaze, #5594.
$150.00 – 200.00

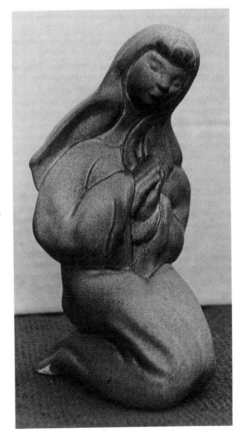

Small flower pot and liner decorated with ivy, #508. *$50.00 – 75.00 set*

16" w., Eagle wall plaque, #5904. *$100.00 – 150.00*

14", Wall shell pocket planter, #4621. *$175.00 – 250.00*

Ashtray/plaque, featuring Afghan, #5332. *$75.00 – 125.00*

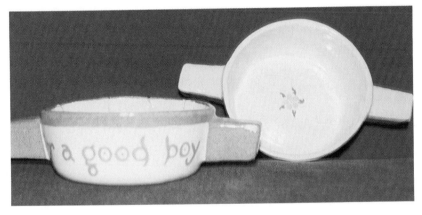

Baby cereal bowls, ready for a hungry little boy, #506. *$75.00 – 125.00 each*

Sea urchin wall plaque, #5670. *$100.00 – 150.00*

17" each, Persian Hunter, #5160, and Persian Lady, #5161. Signed and decorated by Kay. Dated 1951. *$2,000.00 – 2,500.00 pair*

Detail of bird and tether in Persian Hunter's hand.

8", Bust of Chinese princess, circa 1941. *NPA*

Peasant woman figure, early piece, circa 1937. *$1,000.00 – 1,800.00*

Large Godey Lady, #122.
*$300.00 – 400.00 pair with Godey
Man*

Back shows fine detail.

9½", Godey Lady with cape, #122c. The
large Godey Lady is not usually found
with cape.

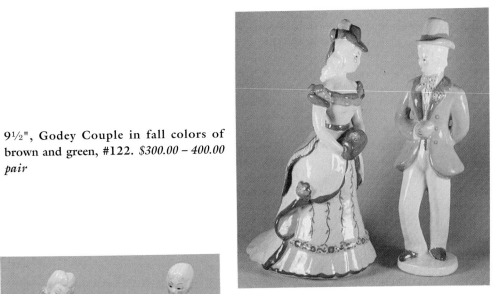

9½", Godey Couple in fall colors of brown and green, #122. *$300.00 – 400.00 pair*

9½", Godey Couple, summer colors, #122. *$300.00 – 400.00 pair*

Godey grouping, back pair, #122, *$300.00 – 400.00 pair*; front pair, #160, *$150.00 – 200.00 pair*; dog, #156. *$100.00 – 125.00*

8", Waving girls with hair detail, may be named "Susan," #5551. *$150.00 – 200.00 each*

7½", Godey Couple, #160. *$150.00 – 200.00 pair*

6", Variations of detail on peasant boys and girls, #113 and #117. *$150.00 – 200.00 pair*

6", Peasant boy and girl, #113 and #117. *$150.00 – 200.00 pair*

Goody, #5014; Casey Jones Jr., #5013, with Engine #9, #5015. *$300.00 – 400.00 set of three*

5", Little girl, "P.J.," with pigtails, #5002. *$150.00 – 200.00*

5" and 7", Choir boys, #210 and #211. *$125.00 – 175.00 each*

6½", Bride and groom, perfect wedding cake toppers, #201 and #204. *$400.00 – 500.00 pair*

10", Grecian wall plaque from Kay's home, #5021. *$200.00 – 250.00*

23" h., Chinese Princess, #477.
$1,500.00 – 2,000.00

13" h., St. Francis, #5457.
$200.00 – 250.00

Detail of Chinese Princess.

18" h., Chinese ancestor, man, tan matte glaze, #5711. *$400.00 – 500.00*

South Seas woman and child, decorated by Kay, #4913. *$300.00 – 350.00*

Chinese Sage and Maiden, #4854 and #4855. *$200.00 – 250.00 pair*

Indian mother, #206, and child, #207. Samples done by Kay in terra cotta to simulate original Indian clay. *$350.00 – 450.00 set of two*

9½", Modjeska award, named for Madame Helena Modjeska, a Polish actress who settled in Orange County. Given each year to local actors in one-act plays staged by the Santa Ana Community Players from 1949 to the late 1950s. *NPA*

17", Mrs. Foo. *$250.00 – 350.00*

5", Scandie boy and girl, #126 and #127. originally listed as Peasant Tots. *$175.00 – 225.00 pair*

5¼", Scandie girl, a Kay Finch Russian variation signed by the artist and dated 1940. Part of a group of ethnic figures with head trays for small flowers, #126. Rare. *$200.000 – 300.00*

Chinese court lady, #401, *$150.00 – 250.00.* Two-piece flower ring, #T506. *$50.00 – 75.00*

11", Court lord #451, and ladies, #400 and #401. *$600.00 – 800.00 set of three*

10½", Chinese court group, in solid colors, #451, #400 and #401. *$450.00 – 650.00 set of three*

10", Chinese court lady, *$150.00 – 250.00*; with 6" fountain and bird, #400. *$100.00 – 125.00*

10½", Chinese court lady in deep turquoise, #402. *$125.00 – 175.00*

24" h., St. Francis. Face and hands are done in bisque, #5456. *$1,200.00 – 1,500.00*

Detail of St. Francis figure.

Original bust of girl. *NPA*

32" h., Merbaby, #4618, and shell basin, #6061, in celadon green. *$1,500.00 – 2,000.00*

Sailor, made by Kay for friends who knew someone at sea, 1943. *NPA*

"Spooners" spoon rest for kitchen use. $200.00 – 250.00

3' h., Chinese Princess, $3,000.00 – 6,000.00

Detail of Chinese Princess.

Original sculpture of mermaid. *NPA*

Chinese Princess with crown.
$4,000.00 – 6,000.00

Christmas figure. *NPA*

6½", Miniature manger, #4952.
$250.00 – 350.00 set

16", Santa personalized charger plate,
#5680. $400.00 – 500.00

11", Special personalized and signed Santa
candy jar, circa 1960, dated last year of studio production. Very rare. $500.00 – 700.00

Santa wall plaque, #5373.
$250.00 – 350.00

Santa punch bowl set,
#5952, 9-piece set.
$600.00 – 800.00

5", Santa mug with cap,
#4950. *$150.00 – 200.00*

4", Santa mug produced in white, gold, and fully decorated, #4950. *$75.00 – 125.00*

Punch bowl, #4951, and set of ten cups, #4975, in luster with gold. *$600.00 – 800.00*

10" Santa sackholder, made for only three years, #5975. Interesting piece, not often found. *$600.00 – 800.00*

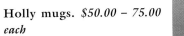

Holly mugs. *$50.00 – 75.00 each*

4½", Holly wreath coasters, #5386, and picture frame, #5372. *$75.00 – 100.00 each*

Bell pattern Christmas punch cup, #5793. Matches 1957 annual Christmas plate. *$50.00 – 75.00 each*

2" to 4", Christmas bells, #6055 and #6056. *$100.00 – 150.00 each*

Christmas plates, clockwise from top left, 1950, 1954, 1953, 1952. *$100.00 – 150.00 each*

Christmas plates, clockwise from top left, 1958, 1960, 1955, 1957. *$100.00 – 150.00 each*

1¼" to 2¼", Miniature angels, #4952. *$75.00 – 100.00 each*

2¾", Cherub head, #212, with 3", large Christmas cup. *$75.00 – 125.00 each*

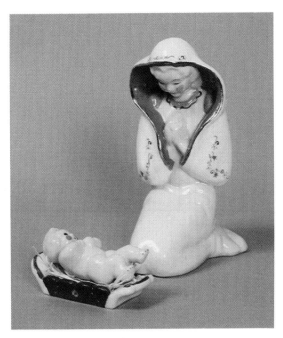

5", Madonna and 1¼" babe in creche, #4900 and #4900a. *$250.00 – 350.00 three piece set*

Nativity tableaux in thatched, wooden stable. Madonna, babe in creche and smallest angel, decorated and signed by Kay Finch. Special display. *NPA*

4", Three popular angels, #114a, b, and c. *$75.00 – 100.00 each*

7", Personalized Christmas tree/candle tree, #T5073. *$150.00 – 200.00*

Three of the same angels produced over the years. Left to right, 1937, 1943, and 1948. *$75.00 – 100.00 each*

Angel, #4802. *$150.00 – 200.00*

1962 Christmas plate. Last in the series. *NPA*

19" l., Sectional three-piece candy cane planter, #509. *$50.00 – 75.00*

Angel candle holder, circa 1941. Beautifully decorated. *$500.00 – 750.00*

Small angel, #4803, and member of angel band, #5153. *$100.00 – 150.00 each*

9", Canister, #5109. *$75.00 – 125.00*

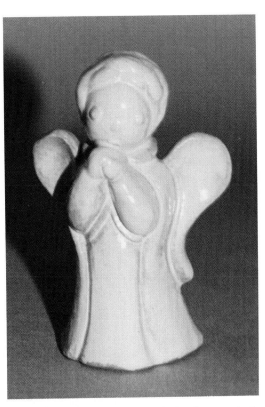

Original angel, 1938. One of the first made in Smokehouse Studio, Santa Ana. *NPA*

Angel band, #5151, #5152, #5153 and 5154. *$400.00 – 450.00 four-piece set*

Girl and boy angels, #4909 and #4910. *$175.00 – 225.00 pair*

Turkey tureen in tanbark and gold, #5361, and salt and pepper shakers, #5362. *$300.00 – 350.00 set*

10", Turkey tureen in silver/white, #5361, with two shakers, #5362. *$350.00 – 400.00 set of three w/ladle*

10", Turkey, #5360, *$250.00 – 350.00,* and small turkey, #4853. *$100.00 – 175.00*

Baby's First from California line, book planter, #6030, with lamb, and with kitten Jezzy. 6½", Bootees, #6035. *$100.00 – 150.00 each*

Baby's First from California line, 6½", baby block planters with baby, bunny, puppy, and bear. *$100.00 – 150.00 each*

Special box from Kay. *NPA*

Heart box, #5051. *$50.00 – 75.00*

Valentine's box with doves, 1955 special. *NPA*

Heart birthday box, personalized to friend Jessie, #5051. *NPA*

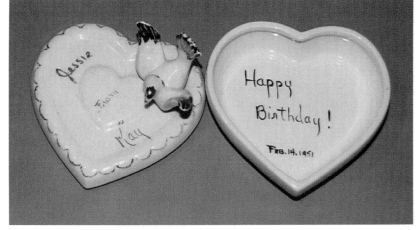

16", Hibiscus canapé platter, #5414. *$150.00 – 200.00*

6" each, Two jacket bunnies: male, #5005, and female with flower hat, #5005b. *$150.00 – 200.00 each*

Bear planter, #4908. *$400.00 – 500.00*

Ceramic banks. *$200.00 – 400.00 each*

Pink pearl swan planters, #4956 and baby, #4958. *$75.00 – 125.00 each*

6¾", Leaf-shaped planter, #205, with owl, #189, both in tanbark. *$75.00 – 100.00 each*

12¼", Large sand-colored flagon with stopper. *$175.00 – 225.00*

10½", Leaf vases in light gray and celadon green with platinum trim. *$50.00 – 75.00 each*

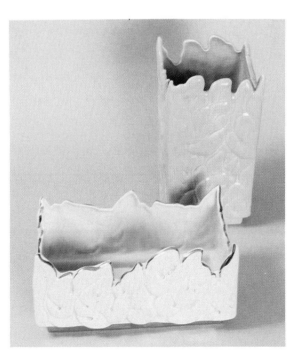

11½" x 10", Sea shell dish, #5114, in yellow/tanbark, with 4" matching fish, #5008. *$100.00 – 150.00 each*

8", Moon vase, #5967. *$150.00 – 200.00*

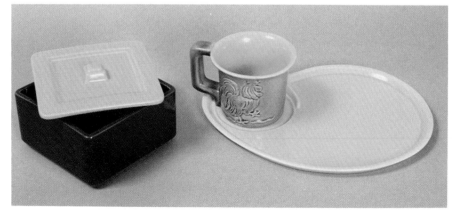

Two-tone square, covered box and snack tray with cup, #5106 and #5107. *$50.00 – 75.00 each*

6" x 5", Vases, celadon green with simulated wooden feet, and orange, #5312. *$50.00 – 75.00 each*

10", Square scalloped bowl, #4657. *$75.00 – 100.00*

Selection of vases, 6" x 5", #5176; two versions of #4653; and 4¼", tanbark and gold, #479. *$50.00 – 75.00 each*

5¾", Swan planter resting on 17" x 11" petal bowl, #5980. Bowl produced for only two years. *$100.00 – 125.00 each*

11½" x 5½", Tanbark flat-top arranger bowl, #5174. *$50.00 – 75.00*

Flower arranger bowl, #5763, and low Ming bowl, #5853. *$50.00 – 75.00 each*

8" h., Matte teakwood patio table lantern in the form of bird feeder. Signed by Kay with matching Mr. and Mrs. Bird, #454 and #453. *$150.00 – 200.00 lantern only*

8½" h., Ming flower urn in orange, #5570. *$50.00 – 75.00*

7", Low pillow bowl, #5762. *$50.00 – 75.00*

Biddy and Butch plate, Buffet ware, #4750. *$75.00 – 100.00*

6½", Hand-painted rooster plate. From a set of dishes labeled Buffet ware. Hard to find. #4757. *$50.00 – 75.00*

6½", Hand-painted hen plate. also hard to find. #4757. *$50.00 – 75.00*

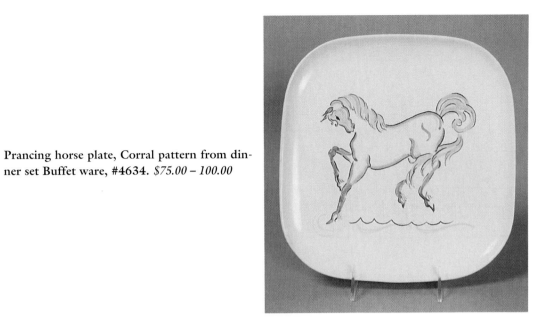

Prancing horse plate, Corral pattern from dinner set Buffet ware, #4634. *$75.00 – 100.00*

Three 6" plates: two elephants personalized and monkey. *$75.00 – 100.00 each*

10", Salad plate featuring vegetable designs, part of a luncheon set, #5381. *$50.00 – 75.00*

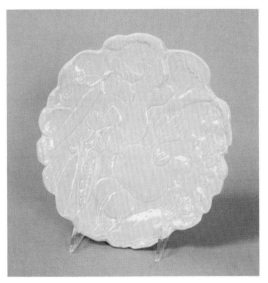

Briar Rose dinnerware pattern: plate, *$50.00 – 75.00 each*; cup and saucer, *$60.00 – 75.00 each*, creamer and sugar, *$125.00 – 200.00 pair w/lid*

Two Briar Rose candleholders, 5¾" on square base, 2" tall. Made by Kay from saucers with handmade leaves and roses applied. Never cast or reproduced, they hold candles from Kay's 85th birthday in 1988. *NPA*

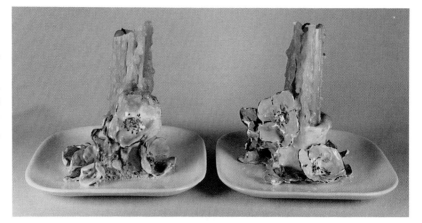

Blue Daisy dinnerware pattern, #4634 – #4638: plate, *$50.00 – 75.00 each*; cup and saucer, *$60.00 – 75.00 each*; creamer and sugar, *$125.00 – 200.00 pair w/lid*; table planter, *$60.00 – 80.00*

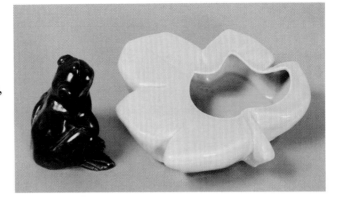

Frog #5009, and leaf planter, #206. *$100.00 – 150.00 each*

Vase, Calico pattern, #4653. *$75.00 – 100.00*

Turquoise bowl, #4658. *$75.00 – 100.00*

Three advertising pieces: 5" two Missouri Mule Mugs, one with original sticker; and ashtray for Trader Island, 5¼" diameter. *$75.00 – 100.00 each*

Assorted dishes: 4", Shells, #510; Oriental fan, #4960; and 7" x 5", soap dish; #5405. *$50.00 – 75.00 each*

3" x 1½", Square decorated flower pots, #508, *$50.00 – 75.00 each*, and two-tone cup, #4766. *$40.00 – 50.00*

9", Large lidded jar, #5961, and low jar, #6020, both bathroom accessories. *$50.00 – 75.00 each*

Two Afghan tumblers in tanbark. *$100.00 – 150.00 each*

Two-tone vase, #4659, flanked by cups, #4766. *$100.00 – 150.00 set*

6½" x 5¼", Wall pocket planter.
$50.00 – 75.00

Small flower pot and base, #508.
$50.00 – 75.00

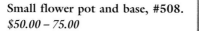

3½", Laughing frog, pale pink matte
variation of the little frog, #5509.
$100.00 – 150.00

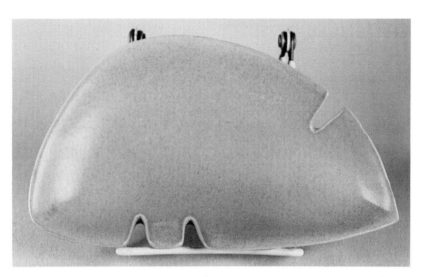

7", Ashtray, probably early 1960s. Identification number unknown. *$25.00 – 35.00*

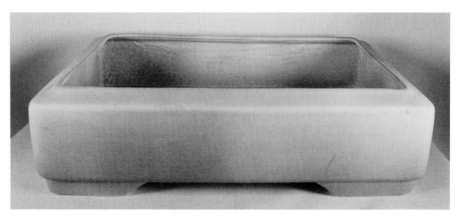

13" x 9", Dwarf tree planter in sand matte glaze, #5572. *$50.00 – 75.00*

11", Bird bath bowl, #5611, *$50.00 – 75.00*, with Mr. Bird, #453, in sand tones.

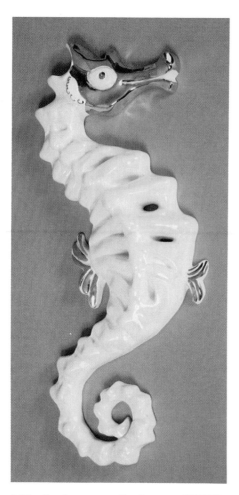

Russian barn bank, #4627. *$300.00 – 350.00*

16", Seahorse wall plaque, #5788.
$100.00 – 150.00

Two dog head ashtrays,
#4773 and #4767.
$100.00 – 150.00 each

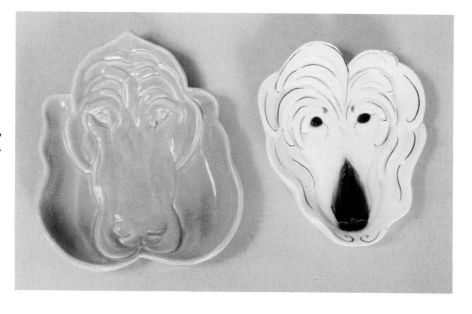

4¾", Parade of Champions plaques, #4955. Shown here, clockwise from top left, boxer, Afghan, Bedlington, Pekingese, bulldog and dachshund; many others made. *$50.00 – 75.00 each*

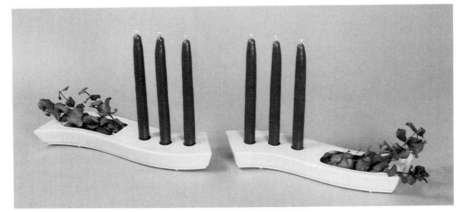

11½" l., Ribbon candle-holders, #203. *$30.00 – 50.00 pair*

Dog mug, personalized. *$75.00 – 100.00*

13" x 9", Tanbark flower arranger bowl on gold runners, #5310, *$75.00 – 100.00*, with tanbark and green fish in center, #5008. *$100.00 – 150.00*

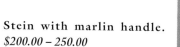

Stein with marlin handle. *$200.00 – 250.00*

3", Baby quail #5985, and soap dish, #5405. *$75.00 – 100.00 each*

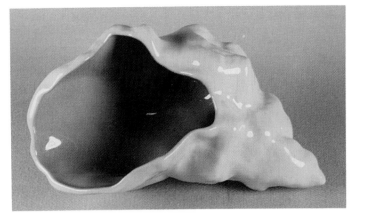

2¾", Sea shell ashtray, #462.
$50.00 – 100.00

Sea shell dish, #5114, and
2" sea babies, #162.
*$150.00 – 175.00 each
(babies only)*

5¾" h., Swan planter with Oriental
motif candleholder/planter, 3¾" l.
$100.00 – 125.00 each

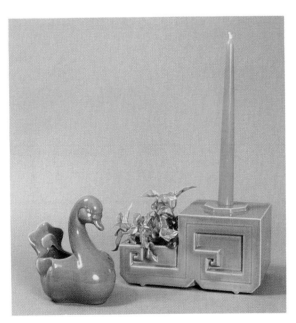

Standing Afghan, #5016, and baby potty, #B107. *$150.00 – 200.00 each*

Canister set, #5108 – 5110. *$200.00 – 350.00 set of five*

Large Crown Crest Afghan tray. *$250.00 – 300.00*

Limited edition bronze Afghan. *$750.00 – 1,000.00*

Studio plate done by a friend. *NPA*

Original sculptures of Kay and Braden on their favorite horses, 1944. *NPA*

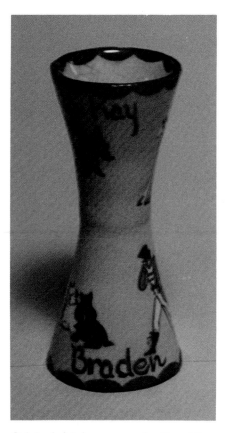

Altered Peanuts to smaller Violet. *NPA*

Original drink measure, by Kay. Circa
1944. *NPA*

First Manker Horses,
late 1930s. *NPA*

Kay Finch, full signature.

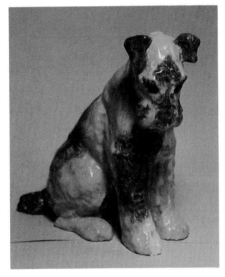

Original 1924 sculpture of Airedale named Mac. *NPA*

Bronze seal and pup, circa 1970. *NPA*

Original heart frame. *NPA*

Prototype 1945 and production 1946 plate of Briar Rose dinnerware pattern, #4634. *NPA*

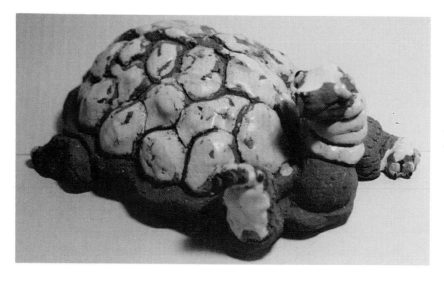

Original terra cotta turtle. *NPA*

Medal awarded to Issy Hiner to commemorate her assistance in the capture of thieves. *NPA*

Tile showing Kay Finch slip colors. *NPA*

Original oil portrait of Kay Finch by Jean Goodwin.
NPA

Original Sculpture of children on horse, circa 1944. *NPA*

4", Original Irish Setter, 1962. *NPA*

Original Christmas sculpture, 1944. *NPA*

Original ceramic tile made for Finch home at 344 Hazel Drive. *NPA*

Parakeet, #5164. *$200.00 – 250.00*

Original wax sculpture for kangaroo, bronze. *NPA*

Original cement sculpture/fountain
of son Cabell. *NPA*

Original sculpture of son George.
NPA

Original perfume bottle of small pup. *NPA*

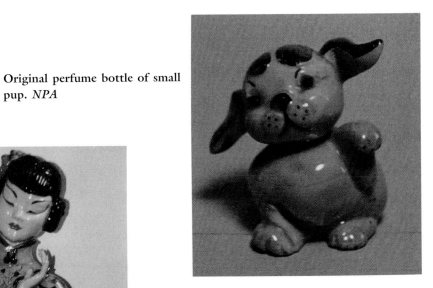

36", Chinese Princess, *$3,000.00+*

Afghan head in bronze relief. Signed by Kay, dated 1979. One of only five made. *NPA*

Aquarius zodiac sign to Jessie Hill.
$100.00 – 150.00 each

Inkwell set, made for
Braden Finch. *NPA*

2", Original clay sculpture of teddy
bear. *NPA*

Original sculpture of cocker, Vicki.
NPA

Field mouse in white. *NPA*

Original sculpture, jewelry box, "Interlude." *NPA*

Original sculpture of cherub. *NPA*

Original sculpture, Band Wagon. *NPA*

Detail of Kay and Braden on the Band Wagon.

Personalized party platter with pachyderm, 1953. *$150.00 – 200.00*

Early ceramic horse. *NPA*

19" l. x 12" h., Lion, #811. *$600.00 – 700.00* (Freeman McFarlin)

Gold-leaf Shih Tzu, #837, and 12½" x 11 ¼", cocker spaniel, #843. *$350.00 – 450.00 each* (Freeman McFarlin)

Gold-leaf poodle and reclining Yorky in silver-leaf, #831. *$550.00 – 650.00 each* (Freeman McFarlin)

12½" x 11 ¾", Cocker Spaniel, #843. *$350.00 – 450.00* (Freeman McFarlin)

Owls: 8½", Hoot owl, #815. *$100.00 – 125.00.* 6", Toot owl, #816. *$50.00 – 75.00* (Freeman McFarlin)

23", Mr. and Mrs. Foo in gold leaf. *$200.00 – 300.00 each* (Freeman McFarlin)

Rabbits, #829 and #830. *$300.00 – 400.00 each* (Freeman McFarlin)

Reclining cat in gold leaf, #833. *$250.00 – 350.00* (Freeman McFarlin)

7½", Gold-leaf giraffe #835, and 6½", Lion bookend in gold leaf. *$200.00 – 250.00 each* (Freeman McFarlin)

12", Whippets or small Greyhounds, in gold leaf and white, #836. *$450.00 – 550.00 each* (Freeman McFarlin)

Afghan (Rudiki), #834. *$600.00 – 700.00* (Freeman McFarlin)

Hen, #841, and Rooster, #840. *$250.00 – 300.00 pair* (Freeman McFarlin)

Duck, #827. *$200.00 – 250.00* (Freeman McFarlin)

Duck, #818. *$200.00 – 250.00* (Freeman McFarlin)

Poodle in silver leaf. *$550.00 – 650.00* (Free-man McFarlin)

Horse. *$300.00 – 400.00* (Freeman McFarlin)

Donkey, #839, with Burro, #475. *$250.00 – 300.00 each* (Freeman McFarlin)

5½", Yorky tile. *$50.00 – 75.00* (Freeman McFarlin)

Owl wall plaque, #825. *$150.00 – 200.00* (Freeman McFarlin)

Mr. Bird and two sizes, #825. Smaller birds *$40.00 – 60.00 each* (Freeman McFarlin)

Gold birds, #825 and #826. *$40.00 – 60.00* (Freeman McFarlin)

Kay Finch CERAMICS

CORONA DEL MAR CALIFORNIA

One of the first catalogs, circa 1940 – 1941.

Pigs in the Parlor

America's most famous family of pottery pigs. Plump pink porkers decorated with freehand color sketches of California's famed flowers in Kay Finch's gorgeous pastels. Each one, from Grandpa to Baby, wears a jolly expression that says, "Take me home". Grandpa, the big pig in the picture below, is 16 inches from the tip of his snout to his tail. Others in proportion.

Top row, left .... Greedy ..No. 165, each......$ 7.50
Top row, right........ Smiley ....No. 164, each......$ 7.50
Tot row, center ...... Baby ......No. 131, dozen....$ 6.00
Bottom row, corners Sassy ......No. 166 each ......$ 3.50
Bottom row, center.. Grandpa .No. 163 each $35.00

Winkie Pig, a newcomer, is not shown in the picture. He is the same size and price as Sassy, and has a fat little face with a sly little wink.

All Prices Retail With Usual Discount to Dealers

Three Little Kittens

Introducing three of the cutest kittens that ever purred in pottery - - - Mehitable No. 181 is in the upper left corner. Hannibal, No. 180, 10 inches tall, has his tail in the air. Jezebel, No. 179, is curled up in the upper right corner. In three color combinations - - - tawney tan, twilight grey, and the popular pastel blues and pinks. Each kitten, $7.50.

Biddy , Butch and babes

There's appeal in this pottery poultry. Biddy, the little mother, pairs off nicely with the rooster, Butch, slightly more than eight inches high. They come in white and green or barnyard yellow and brown. Butch, No. 176, is $5.50 and Biddy, No. 177, is $5.00. The chicks are $6.00 a dozen.

Chinese Ladies of the Court

Fascinating in the robes of ancient Empresses, these porcelain type glaze figures are among the finest of the kind made.

The face and hands are of Cathay bisque and each hand is individually modeled.

Delicate authentic patterns and subtle irridescent colors. Ten and one-half inches.

Left, No. 400 and right, No. 401. Each, $15.00

Wall Brackets in Lotus Flower pattern for Chinese ladies. Each $2.50

Little Angels that are Heavenly

Three matched angels in different poses. Four inches high. Left to right, 114b, 114c and 114a. Dozen, $9.00.

Topsy-turvy seraphs. One on head and the other is shocked. Left to right, 140b and 140a. Dozen, $6.00

Peasant Children ❧ Godey Couple ❧ Scandi Tots

The charm of Europe lives again in these colorful children with their multi-colored garb and quaint hats and hair-do's. Six and one-half inches. No. 113. Pair $5.00.

Truly American are these dainty visitors from the Godey book. No. 160 seven-inch size, $10.00 pair. No. 122, nine-inch size without cape, $15.00 pair. With cape, No. 122a, $17.00 pair.

Russia and the peasants of Scandinavia inspired these demure children. Boy holds pig. Girl wears shawl. Many colors. No. 126, Pair, $4.00.

Seafarers from the Studio by the Sea

FROM her studio overlooking the blue Pacific ocean, Kay Finch drew the desire to model these pieces in the greens, blues and golds of seawater with the pale pinks of pastel pottery. Upper corners. Sea Baby with fish's tail. No. 162, $1.00 each. Center, Mermaid, No. 161, six inches, $2.50. Papa Turtle, No. 125, $1.00. Baby Turtle, No. 126, 50c. Guppies, many colors, two shapes, No. 173, dozen, $9.00.

Persian & Peke

In pink, rose and white, these pets are spectacular. Big cat, No. 155, 10½ inches high, $15.00 each. Big dog, No. 154, lying down, $15.00 each. Yorkshire pups, $7.50 each. Small cat and dog, No. 157 and 156 respectively, each $1.25.

Cock & Pheasant

These stately birds bear a full panoply of brightly colored feathers, perhaps the most brilliant of the line.

Cock, No. 129, eleven inches, $10.00 each.

Pheasant, No. 153, $15.00 each.

Lamb with Garland

Lifesize, this big lamb has as much personality as its original.

In pink and white with a collar of colorful blossoms, No. 167, $45.00.

The smaller prancing lamb comes in pink and white or all white, No. 168, 10 inches high, each $10.00.

Containers

Something different in shape and decoration! That is why these new numbers have hit.

Picture to left, upper half, flower or cigarete vase, assorted designs and colors. No. 508, dozen $14.40. Lower half, shell dish, two-tone combination. No. 510. dozen, $14.40.

Below to left, four-sided pot with relief pattern. In celadon, white on pink, green on white, sea-green on grey. No. 509. each $3.00.

Below to right, round cache pots with relief design. In white with green or pink with rose and brown. No. 504. for 4-inch pot, each $3.50. No. 505 for 3-inch pot, each $2.50

Baby Cup

"For a Good Boy" and "For a Good Girl" cups and bowls in delicate pink with blue or rose lettering. Cups, No. 507, each $1.50. Bowls, No. 506, each $2.00.

Ducky

Sleek little ducks in three color combinations, sand - - - white - - - or yellow with corresponding trim. No. 178, pair, $3.00.

Animal Kingdom

109 —Standing lamb, 5½ in., ea....$1.50
109b—Same with collar and
        bow, each $2.00
136 —Kneeling lamb, each.............$1.00
135 —Donkey, each.......................$2.00
110 —Circus horse, white with col-
        ored mane and tail, each.......$1.50
120 —Mama rabbit, white, 4-in., ea...$1.50
121 —Baby bunnies, 1½-in., each.... .50
152 —Cottontail, pink and blue, ea..$2.00
108 —Squirrels, brown and white,
        each $1.50
130 —Percherons, pink with colored
        mane & tail, three poses, ea...$1.50

A Message to New Customers

IF you are not able to visit the showrooms of our representatives to make a personal selection and wish to try a small initial order, may we suggest the following combination of tested sellers. This combination may be added to by selections from the catalogue.

Peasants, No. 113, pair	$5.00	Baby cup, No. 507, one	1.50
Sassy pig	3.50	Horse, No. 110 or 130, one	1.50
Vase, No. 508, three	3.60		
Baby pig, No. 131, three	1.50		19.60
Guppy, No. 173, one	.75	Packing	.40
Small cat, No. 157, one	1.25		
Sea Baby, No. 162, one	1.00	Total	$20.00

Retail prices shown. Usual discount to dealers. F.O.B. Corona del Mar, Calif.

Terms:

All prices shown here are retail. Usual discount to dealers. Terms: Two per cent discount if paid within 10 days from date of invoice. Net amount due in 30 days. Check should accompany initial mail orders. Three references required for opening of an account.

Shipping:

All shipping is f.o.b. Corona del Mar, Calif. A packing charge of two per cent is made, with a minimum of 25c. Merchandise shipped by customer's choice route. Any breakage claims must be filed by customer with transportation company.

Kay Finch Ceramics

Corona del Mar, Calif.
121 Coast Highway   Ph. Newport Beach 2359

1946 Kay Finch

CERAMICS

CORONA DEL MAR, CALIFORNIA.

Kay Finch CERAMICS

... created in California beside the blue Pacific at Corona del Mar. This world-famous artist was born in Texas and is as American as the United States flag. Kay started sculpturing when a tiny child ... an art student later in the South ... and a traveler in Europe and the Orient. Her sources of inspiration are boundless and rich. She can turn her hand to any subject and make it live. Let the pages of this catalogue show you dreams that have come true through the talented fingers of Kay Finch, outstanding producer of artware pottery now famous throughout the world.

CALIFORNIA COUNTRY
BREAKFAST SETS

Newest addition to the extensive collection of individual Kay Finch creations. Pink pottery body with Flower pattern on a delicate sea-green background. Choice of Briar Rose or Blue Daisy.

4634 . . . **PLATE**—10½ inches
across . . . Retail price each 5.50

4635 . . . **CUP**—3 inches across, 2¾ inches high . . . and **4636** . . . **SAUCER**— 6 inches across.
Retail price together . . . 5.50

4637 . . . **CREAMER**—3 inches
across . . . Retail price each 4.50

4638 . . . **SUGAR BOWL**—3 inches
across . . . Retail price each 5.50

4634

4637

4638

4635 - 4636

4634

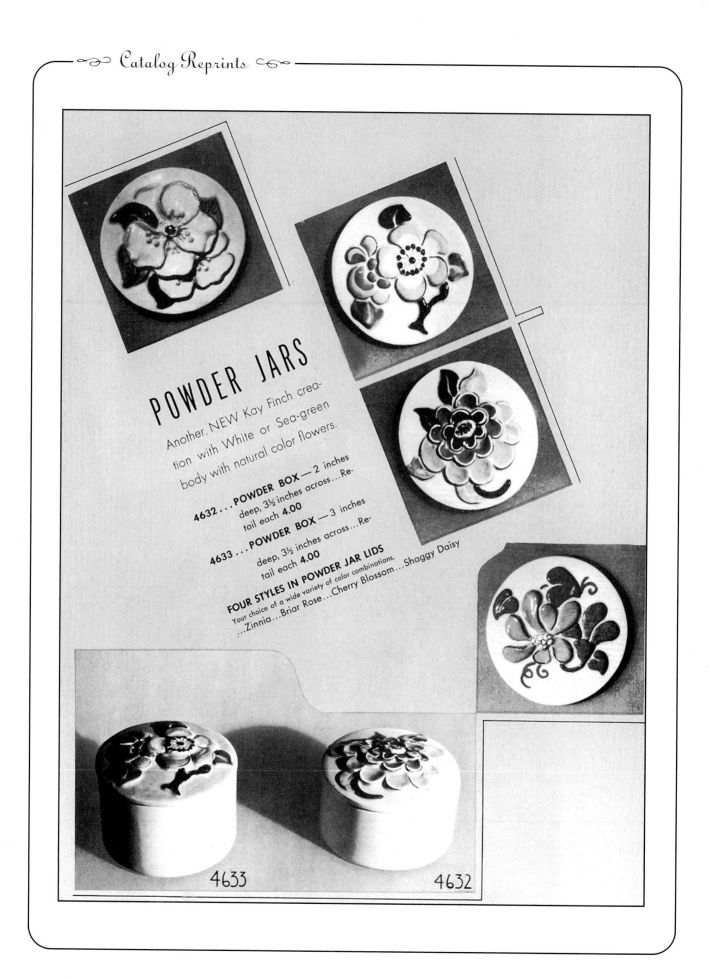

POWDER JARS

Another. NEW Kay Finch creation with White or Sea-green body with natural color flowers.

4632 . . . **POWDER BOX**—2 inches deep, 3½ inches across . . . Retail each **4.00**

4633 . . . **POWDER BOX**—3 inches deep, 3½ inches across . . . Retail each **4.00**

FOUR STYLES IN POWDER JAR LIDS
Your choice of a wide variety of color combinations.
. . . Zinnia . . . Briar Rose . . . Cherry Blossom . . . Shaggy Daisy

4633   4632

SEA SHELL FAMILY

4618 . . . WATER BABY—31 inches
tall, in glowing sea greens
and pastel shades on a
beautiful sculptured base.
Can be used as fountain
or flower holder.
Retail price each 250.00

4621 . . . WALL SHELL POCKET—
14 inches tall. Greens and
Pinks . . . Retail price each 25.00

463 . . . SHELL VASE & WALL POCKET
4¾ inches high . . .
Retail price each 4.00

4620 . . . COCKLE SHELL—23 inches
across. Pink with choice of
pastel inside . . . Retail each 45.00

4619 . . . CONCH SHELL—12 inches
high. Pink with choice of
pastel inside . . . Retail each 25.00

462 . . . SHELL ASHTRAY—2¾ in.
high . . . Retail price each 1.50

461 . . . SHELL MATCH HOLDER—
2 in. high Pink with colored lining
. . . Retail price each 1.20

510 . . . SHELL DISHES—4 inches
across . . . Retail price each 1.20

CHINESE GROUP

Delicate original designs done with exquisite care and taste in the famous Kay Finch pastels.

4629 . . . CHINESE BOY—
7½ inches high   7.50

4630 . . . CHINESE GIRL—
7½ inches high   7.50

4631 . . . LITTLE DUCK—Sold only with Chinese Boy and Girl as a group . . . No extra charge.

400 . . . COURT LADY — 10½ inches tall . . Exquisite pastels. Retail price, ea. 15.00

401 . . . COURT LADY — 10½ inches tall . . Rich pastels. Retail price each 15.00

451 . . . CHINESE PRINCE 11¼ inches tall, in beautiful pastels . . .
Retail price each 20.00

126 . . . SCANDIE GIRL
5¼ inches tall, in pretty pastels.
Retail price each 3.50

127 . . . SCANDIE BOY
5¼ inches tall, in same pastels.
Retail price each 3.50

113 . . . PEASANT BOY
6¾ inches tall, rich pastels.
Retail price each 3.75

117 . . . PEASANT GIRL
6¾ inches tall, matching pastels.
Retail price each 3.75

122 . . . GODEY MAN & LADY
9½ inches tall. Soft pastels.
Retail Pair 20.00

122C . . . GODEY MAN & LADY
with cape and hats
Retail Pair 22.50

160 . . . GODEY MAN & LADY
7½ inches tall, exquisite pastels
Retail Pair 12.50

4611 . . . ENGLISH VILLAGE BANK
5½ inches tall, Kay Finch pastels.
Retail price each 7.50

4610 . . . CHURCH BANK
6¾ inches high, in exquisite pastels.
Retail price each 7.50

4612 . . . VICTORIAN HOUSE BANK
5½ inches tall, lovely pastels.
Retail price each 7.50

4628 . . . SWISS CHALET BANK
6 inches tall, beautiful pastels.
Retail price each 7.50

4627 . . . RUSSIAN BARN BANK
4 inches tall, enchanting pastel colors.
Retail price each 7.50

212 . . . CHERUB HEAD
2¾ inches high. Kay Finch pastels.
Retail price each 2.50

114 . . . ANGELS
4¼ inches tall, in angelic pastels.
Retail price each 2.00

210 . . . CHOIR BOY
Standing 7½ inches tall, rich pastels.
Retail price each 5.00

211 . . . CHOIR BOY
Kneeling, 5½ inches tall, rich pastels.
Retail price each 5.00

204 . . . GROOM
6½ inches tall in fine deep pastels.
Retail price each 7.50

201 . . . BRIDE
6½ inches tall in white and soft pastels.
Retail price each 12.50

KAY FINCH DOGS

in almost life size models they express most
enchantingly their dogginess in a smooth
and decorative style.

170 and 171 . . . YORKY PUPS—5½ and 6 inches high.
Soft pastels. Retail pair 15.00

465 . . . POMERANIAN "MITZI"—10 inches high.
Captivating pastels. Retail each 25.00

159 . . . COACH DOG—17½ inches tall, natural
coloring. Retail price each 45.00

KAY FINCH DOGS

in a variety of almost life size models that prove them irresistibly tempting and friendly.

158 . . . **YORKSHIRE TERRIER** — known as "Puddin" 11 inches high. Soft coloring. Retail price each 35.00

154 . . . **PEKINESE** — 14 inches long in captivating pastels. Retail price each 15.00

455 . . . **COCKER "VICKI"** 11¾ inches high . . . Soft, rich pastels. Retail price each 35.00

FEATHERED FRIENDS

Typical of the artistry and charm of Kay Finch original designs in a commanding selection to choose from.

187 . . . LARGE OWL "HOOT"
8¾ inches high in pastels and grays.
Retail each 8.00

189 . . . SMALL OWL "TOOTSIE"
3¾ inches high in pastels and grays.
Retail each 2.00

188 . . . OWL "TOOT"
5¾ inches high in pastels and grays.
Retail each 4.00

468 . . . PENGUIN "PEE WEE"
3¼ inches high. Natural coloring.
Retail each 2.00

467 . . . PENGUIN "POLLY"
4¾ inches high. Natural coloring.
Retail each 3.00

466 . . . PENGUIN "PETE"
7½ inches high. Natural coloring.
Retail each 6.50

177-176 . . . BIDDY AND BUTCH
8¼ inches high. White and green . . . Yellow and brown . . . or White and pastels.
Retail each pair 12.50

129 . . . CHANTICLEER
10¾ inches high in many color combinations with greens and purples featured.
Retail price each 15.00

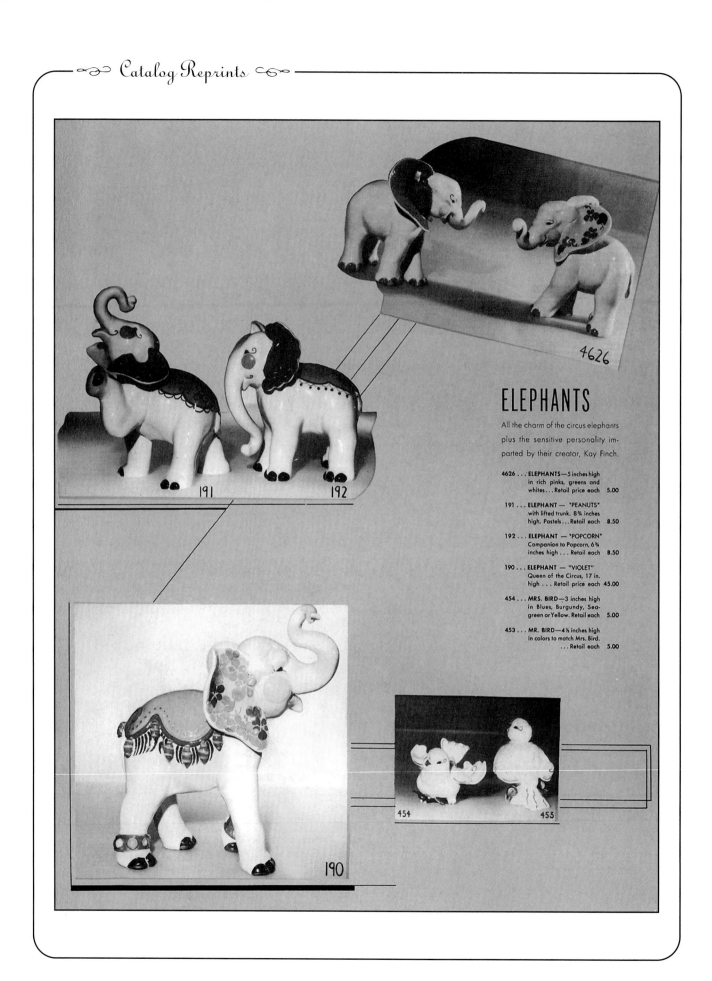

ELEPHANTS

All the charm of the circus elephants plus the sensitive personality imparted by their creator, Kay Finch.

4626 . . . ELEPHANTS—5 inches high in rich pinks, greens and whites . . . Retail price each   5.00

191 . . . ELEPHANT — "PEANUTS" with lifted trunk. 8¾ inches high. Pastels . . . Retail each   8.50

192 . . . ELEPHANT — "POPCORN" Companion to Popcorn, 6¾ inches high . . . Retail each   8.50

190 . . . ELEPHANT — "VIOLET" Queen of the Circus, 17 in. high . . . Retail price each 45.00

454 . . . MRS. BIRD—3 inches high in Blues, Burgundy, Sea-green or Yellow. Retail each   5.00

453 . . . MR. BIRD—4½ inches high in colors to match Mrs. Bird. . . . Retail each   5.00

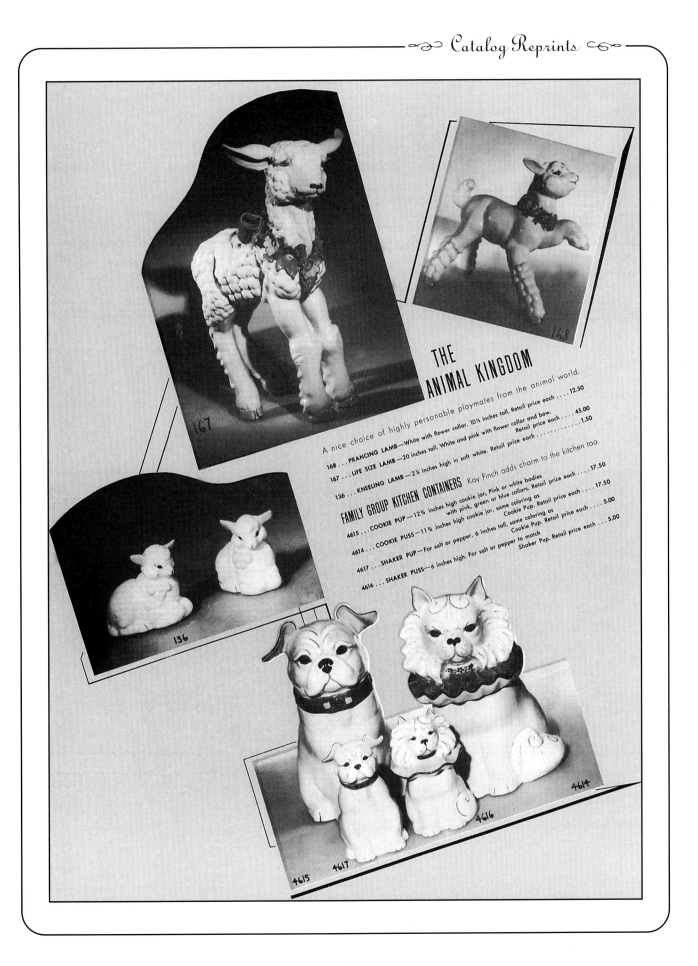

THE ANIMAL KINGDOM

A nice choice of highly personable playmates from the animal world.

168 . . . PRANCING LAMB—White with flower collar. 10½ inches tall. Retail price each 12.50

167 . . . LIFE SIZE LAMB—20 inches tall. White and pink with flower collar and bow.
Retail price each 45.00

136 . . . KNEELING LAMB—2¼ inches high in soft white. Retail price each 1.50

FAMILY GROUP KITCHEN CONTAINERS Kay Finch adds charm to the kitchen too.

4615 . . . COOKIE PUP—12¾ inches high cookie jar, Pink or white bodies
with pink, green or blue collars. Retail price each 17.50

4614 . . . COOKIE PUSS—11¾ inches high cookie jar, same coloring as
Cookie Pup. Retail price each 17.50

4617 . . . SHAKER PUP—For salt or pepper. 6 inches tall, same coloring as
Cookie Pup. Retail price each 5.00

4616 . . . SHAKER PUSS—6 inches high. For salt or pepper to match
Shaker Pup. Retail price each 5.00

CATS IN LOVABLE MOOD

Unusually decorative with fine feline personality and originality

182 . . . **MUFF**—Kitten curled up to sleep. Pastel combinations or grays. 3¼ inches high. Retail price each . . . 2.50

183 . . . **PUFF**—Kitten at play in pastel combinations or grays 3¼ inches high. Retail price each . . . 2.50

155 . . . **"AMBROSIA"**—Persian Cat 10¾ inches tall. Blended pinks and white. Retail price each . . . 15.00

181 . . . **"MEHITABEL"**—Playful Cat in pastels or grays. 8½ inches tall. Retail price each . . . 8.50

180 . . . **"HANNIBAL"**—Angry Cat in pastels or grays 10¼ inches tall. Retail each . . . 8.50

179 . . . **"JEZEBEL"**—Contented Cat in pastels or grays. 6 inches tall. Retail each . . . 8.50

CHOICE PIGS

America's most famous family of pottery Pigs. Plump pink porkers with California blooms.

165 . . . GRUMPY—6 inches high in pink with colorful flowers.
Retail each 8.00

165-B . . . GRUMPY as a Bank.
Retail each 8.50

164 . . . SMILEY—6¾ inches high in pink with gay blossoms.
Retail each 8.00

164-B . . . SMILEY as a Bank.
Retail each 8.50

185 . . . WINKIE—3¾ inches tall in pink with soft blossoms.
Retail each 4.00

185-B . . . WINKIE as a Bank.
Retail each 4.50

166 . . . SASSY—3½ inches tall. Pink with soft blossoms . . . Retail each 4.00

166-B . . . SASSY as a Bank.
Retail each 4.50

163 . . . GRANDPA—10 inches tall. 16 inches long. Pink with California flowers . . . . Retail each 35.00

LOVABLE GIFTS . . . to delight the eye of every beholder!

464 . . . CAMEL—5 inches tall, in grays and tans with pastel accents. Retail price each 4.50

178 . . . DUCKS—"Peep and Jeep" approximately 4 inches high. Rich pastels, white. Retail each 2.00

152 . . . COTTONTAIL BABY—2½ inches high, pink and white. Retail each 2.50

452 . . . LISTENING BUNNY—8½ inches tall, pinks or browns. Retail each 8.50

130 . . . PERCHERONS—(not pictured) In three sizes, 4¼ to 6¾ inches high.
Mane and tail in color. Retail each . . . 2.00

Kay Finch

Kay Finch Ceramics
Corona del Mar, California

KAY FINCH--herself--
has been designing since
she was a little tot. She
studied sculpture and
ceramics in America, and
traveled in Europe and the
Orient to see how it was
done in other lands.

One of California's Oldest and Best Known Ceramic Studios

Since 1935 Kay Finch has been supplying her famous pottery animals and people to lovers of fine ceramics. In the 20 years that have passed since the establishment of the firm, the name Kay Finch Ceramics has come to mean tops in design, quality, good taste, and business reliability.

4776 28" $150

BABY DONKEY
(Lifesize)

"HERITAGE collection"

A number of favorites stand
out among Kay's many creations.
They highlight the charm and
style of this talented artist.
They are listed on both sides
of this sheet to help you start
or add to your collection of
truly "Heritage" ceramics.

4843-4 pair 6.50
MR. & MRS. BANTY

473-452 8¼" ea $10
"CARROTS"·"LISTENER"

4804-5 each $3
MUMBO & JUMBO

152 each $3
COTTONTAIL

4905A-B each $4
DICKY BIRDS

475 BURRO $10

4806 COLT 11" $10

PRICES RETAIL
7-15-58

233

Kay Finch's

Kay Finch Ceramics
Corona del Mar, California

"HERITAGE collection"

Selected favorites in traditional hand-painted
coloring by Kay Finch in pastel slips or lusters

PRICES
RETAIL

Free shipping
in U.S.A. on
orders over
$100 net

182 MUFF $3

179 JEZEBEL $10

183 PUFF $3

5103 SIAMESE $10

108A-B   each $3
SQUIRRELS

185 WINKY $5
166 SASSY $5

453-4   pair $10
MR. & MRS. BIRD

155 AMBROSIA $16.50

5164 BABY AMBROSIA $4
5179-80   ea $2.50
SIAMESE KITTENS

4956 SWAN BOWL $6
4958 BABY SWAN $2
4957 MEDIUM $3.50

187 PAPA $10.00
189 BABY   3.00
188 MAMA   5.00

176-7   pair   16.50   BUTCH & BIDDY

DOVES   5101-2L   pr   27.50

7-15-58

234

EXQUISITE BOWLS
by Kay Finch

entirely new! postwar development!

Kay has been asked so many times for a series of lovely bowls for artistic uses, that it gives her real pleasure to be able NOW to present them to you. Postwar expansion of the Kay Finch Studios at Corona del Mar, California, has made it possible to create bowls in original shapes not to be found elsewhere. All are in semi-vitreous pottery, warranted not to leak. COLORS, are two of Kay Finch's lovliest pastels, very skillfully blended or contrasted to create a decorative two-tone effect under the sheen of a beautiful glaze. A few styles come in hand decorated finishes to match Briar Rose and Blue Daisy patterns in her new "California Country" luncheon ware.

4657—Square Flange Bowl 11 x 11 inches Retail 7.50
4657M—Same Flange Bowl, glaze-metal fin. Retail 8.50
This flange shape is especially good for arrangements where it is desired to place figure on land, but not in the water.
4658—Oval Long Bowl 13¾ by 9 inches . . . . Retail 7.50
4656—Taper Cup 3½ inches tall . . . . . . Retail 2.00
4656M—Same Taper Cup, glaze-metal fin. Retail 3.00
4629—Chinese Boy 19th Century Costume . . . . Retail 7.50
4630—Chinese Girl to match . . . . Retail 7.50
4631—Little Duck – no extra charge with Chinese set above

EXCITING NEWS!

Something Different!

FOR THE FIRST TIME . . .

Kay Finch presents to you

COMBINATION GLAZE POTTERY

AND ACTUAL COPPER BRONZE

OR BRASS PLATING

Using a new process of metal plating developed during the war, Kay Finch can now combine glazes with actual copper, bronze and brass to produce pottery pieces partly glazed and partly metal plated. The brightly burnished brass and antique bronze produce extremely handsome effects. Available in a few shades at slightly higher prices than the two-tone glazes illustrated.

4659—Oblong Flare shape 5¾ inches long . . . . Retail 3.00
4659 H.D.—Same shape, hand dec. with floral pattern Ret. 3.00
4660—Shallow Oblong shape 12 inches long . . . . Retail 4.00

4652—Square Taper shape 4 inches tall . . . . Retail 4.00
4651—Square Taper shape 6¼ inches tall . . . . Retail 5.00
4650—Square Taper shape 9¼ inches tall . . . . Retail 7.50
4650 M—Same shape with metal-glaze finish . . . . Retail 9.00

4653—Oblong Taper shape 6¼ inches tall . . . . Retail 5.00
4653 M—Same shape with metal-glaze finish . . . . Retail 6.50
4654—Oblong Taper shape 4 inches tall . . . . Retail 4.00
4655—Oblong Taper shape 1 7/8 inches tall . . . . Retail 3.00

complete **Kay Finch CERAMICS** line of artware pottery shown by her representatives in the following cities.

LOS ANGELES—Dillon-Wells Inc., 710 W. 7th St., Los Angeles 14, Calif.
CHICAGO—Robert P. Pierce, 1352 Merchandise Mart, Chicago 54, Illinois
NEW YORK CITY—M. Wille Art Goods, 225 Fifth Ave., New York City 10

Glossary

This glossary is to assist the many pottery collectors who are unfamiliar with much of the art terminology used in the ceramic world. It will give the collector a better understanding of what may be found.

Airbrush decoration – The process in which an atomizer is used by employing compressed air and paint in a very fine mist to the fired piece before glazing.

Bisque – Pottery that has been fired for the first time but not glazed.

Body – The consistency, structure of the ceramic piece.

Ceramic – Any object made of clay that is fired with other minerals.

Clay – A fine-grained, firm, natural material, plastic when wet, which becomes hard when fired.

Crackle glaze – The process in which a ceramic object is fired at a higher and faster temperature in the kiln causing a fine network of cracks throughout the glaze.

Engobe – A layer of slip which is applied to alter body color.

Finishing – The process of removing all mold lines and rough edges from cast ceramic before the first firing. If the finishing is not done properly, mold lines will appear in the firing.

Glaze – A smooth, glassy coating on a clay surface. Can be made of silica.

Greenware – Unfired pottery that is dried by natural air.

Kiln furniture – The shelves, cranks, and props used for supporting ware in the kiln.

Leather-hard – The state of clay between plastic and dry.

Luster – A metallic quality of paint produced by the reduction of oxides.

Luting – Joining leather-hard clay pieces using slip.

Master mold – The original mold called the block made from a model .

Modeling – The process of sculpting the original art from which the molds are made for production of ceramic objects.

Mold – The second process in ceramic production: a hollow plaster of Paris form into which liquid or plastic clay is poured.

On-glaze – Decoration applied directly onto the glaze, usually ceramic colors and enamels.

Oxidation – Firing with enough oxygen to ensure complete combustion of all carbonaceous matter, either in the fuel or in the clay.

Periodic kiln – Where pottery is fired/heated in gradual cycles and then allowed to cool before removal from the kiln.

Plasticity – The essential quality of clay, enabling it to be molded.

Relief decoration – Raised, modeled decoration.

Resist – A decoration technique in which selected areas of clay, bisque, or glaze are treated so that they reject the application of slip, color, or glaze.

Scraffito – The decorative process which employs scratching a line through a layer of slip to expose the clay body beneath.

Slip – A form of liquid clay used for decorating. It can be used for binding (luting) to join clay pieces to an unfired figure.

Slip Decoration – Underglaze decorative process in which colored liquid clay is used as a painting medium. Can be tinted many colors.

Talc – A fine-grained mineral which is used in a mixture with clay to give the clay body and a more plastic form.

Tunnel Kiln – A drying apparatus with continuously moving conveyor on which ceramic ware is moved at a very slow pace at varying heat temperatures. May take up to 24 hours for the full process.

Bibliography

Balboa Bay Blade, "Dreams Come True as Former Editor Capitalizes Genius."
   Balboa, CA: April 4, 1947.

Bryant, Kathy, "In the California Mold." *Los Angeles Times*, Section N. Los Angeles, CA:
   Oct. 8, 1994.

California Manufacturer's Directory. *Los Angeles Times Mirror Press*, Los Angeles, CA: 1948.

Chaney, Charles and Stanley Skee. *Plaster Mold and Model Making*.
   New York, NY: Van Nostrand Reinhold Company, 1973.

Chipman, Jack. *Collector's Encyclopedia of California Pottery*.
   Paducah, KY: Collector Books, 1992.

Christian Science Monitor. "American Ceramic Art Takes a Godey Turn."
   Oct. 7, 1941.

Cox, Susan. "The Investigation of a California Artist."
   Collector Magazine, Vol. 14, No. 6, June 1994.

Derwich, Jenny B., "Kay Finch Ceramics."
   Pottery Collectors Newsletter, July-Aug., 1980.

Dutton, Davis. *A California Portfolio, the Golden State in Words and Pictures*.
   Oakland, CA: Westways Book, 1970.

Electrical Times. "Electricity Speeds Making of Kay Finch Ceramics." Nov. 1947.

Frick, Devin. "California Kilns." *Anaheim Museum Catalog*. Anaheim, CA:
   Aug. 24-Nov. 23, 1994.

Giftwares. "An Article is No Better Than Its Quality."
  December, 1994.

Hallan-Gibson, Pamela. *The Golden Promise, An Illustrated History of Orange County.*
  Northridge, CA: Windsor Publications, Inc., 1986.

Hotel del Coronado. *History of a Legend.* Coronado, CA: 1984.

Knoll, Kathleen. *V is for Victory.* New York: Alfred E. Knopf, 1995.

Lehner, Lois. *Lehner's Encyclopedia of U.S. Marks on Pottery, Porcelain & Clay.*
  Paducah, KY: Collector Books, 1988.

Lombard, Dorothy. "An Easter Surprise for the Fabulous Kay Finch." *Our Afghans.*
  Neddle Publications, Canoga Park, CA: VXX, No. 4, April, 1987.

Morgan, Judith and Neil. "Orange a Most California County."
  National Geographic, V. 160, No. 6, Dec. 1981.

Newport Balboa News-Times, "She Knows How." Newport Beach, CA: Oct. 27, 1948.

Newport-Balboa News Times, "Finch Studio At C.D. to Be Coast Show Place."
  Newport Beach, CA: Nov. 13, 1941.

Parker, Marilyn. *Orange County: Indians to Industry.* Orange County Title Co., 1963.

Riverside Press, "Club Hears About Pottery." Riverside, CA: Feb. 12, 1947.

Santa Ana Register, "Corona del Mar Woman Creates Unusual Figures."
  Santa Ana, CA: Aug. 13, 1941.

Santa Paula Chronicle, "Local Artists Inspired Finch Ceramics."
  Santa Paula, CA: Jan. 30, 1941.

"Sascha Brastoff at Anaheim Museum." *Collector Magazine*, Vol. 14, No. 7, July, 1994.

Script. "Art in Industry: Southland Ceramics." Dec. 1947.

Stiles, Helen. *Pottery in the United States.* New York: E. P. Duton and Co., Inc., 1941.

The Antique Trader Weekly, "Kay Finch Ceramics Reach New High."
  Corona del Mar, CA: Nov. 16, 1993.

The Orange County Register, "A Tribute to Kay Finch."
  Santa Ana, CA: March 10, 1994.

Webb, Frances Finch and Jack Webb. *The New Kay Finch Identification Guide.*
  Mountain View, CA: 1996.

Wilson, Nichols Field. "American Ceramist."
  Adventures in Business, Buena Park, CA: Vol. 2, No. 22. Oct. 13, 1944.

Schroeder's
ANTIQUES
Price Guide

. . . is the #1 best-selling antiques & collectibles value guide on the market today, and here's why . . .

Schroeder's ANTIQUES Price Guide

OUR **1** BEST SELLER!

Identification & Values Of Over 50,000 Antiques & Collectibles

8½ x 11, 608 Pages, $12.95

• *More than 300 advisors, well-known dealers, and top-notch collectors work together with our editors to bring you accurate information regarding pricing and identification.*

• *More than 45,000 items in almost 500 categories are listed along with hundreds of sharp original photos that illustrate not only the rare and unusual, but the common, popular collectibles as well.*

• *Each large close-up shot shows important details clearly. Every subject is represented with histories and background information, a feature not found in any of our competitors' publications.*

• *Our editors keep abreast of newly developing trends, often adding several new categories a year as the need arises.*

If it merits the interest of today's collector, you'll find it in *Schroeder's*. And you can feel confident that the information we publish is up to date and accurate. Our advisors thoroughly check each category to spot inconsistencies, listings that may not be entirely reflective of market dealings, and lines too vague to be of merit. Only the best of the lot remains for publication.

Without doubt, you'll find
SCHROEDER'S ANTIQUES PRICE GUIDE
the only one to buy for
reliable information and values.